THE LITTLE GIANT® BOOK
OF
CARD GAMES

By
Alfred Sheinwold,
Sheila Anne Barry, and
Margie Golick

Illustrated by
Myron Miller

STERLING PUBLISHING CO., INC.
NEW YORK

Library of Congress Cataloging-in-Publication Data Available

Published by Sterling Publishing Co., Inc.
387 Park Avenue South, New York, NY 10016

Excerpted from
101 Best Family Card Games © 1992
by Sterling Publishing Co., Inc.
Great Solitaire Games, previously published under the title of
World's Best Card Games for One © 1992
by Sheila Anne Barry
Card Games for Smart Kids © 1998 by Margie Golick;
portions of which were previously published by Pembroke
Publishers Ltd., Markham, Ontario, in *Reading, Writing, and
Rummy* © 1986 by Margie Golick
Distributed in Canada by Sterling Publishing
c/o Canadian Manda Group, One Atlantic Avenue, Suite 105,
Toronto, Ontario, Canada M6K 3E7
Distributed in Great Britain and Europe by Chris Lloyd at
Orca Book Services, Stanley House, Fleets Lane,
Poole BH15 3AJ, England
Distributed in Australia by Capricorn Link (Australia) Pty. Ltd. P.O.
Box 704, Windsor, NSW 2756, Australia

Sterling ISBN 1-4027-0286-8

Contents

What a wonderful rainy-day activity card playing is! It's great to break out the cards when you decide you want a little challenge or to play a game. You can play at home on the living room floor, on the kitchen table, in the car on trips, in the train, on airplanes, or in waiting rooms. Or take them to the farm or the country or the beach.

You may like collecting cards from other countries or places you visit. Souvenir cards often have scenes on the front or back. And some cards have suit markings that are different. In Germany, bears, bells, acorns, and leaves sometimes replace the usual hearts, diamonds, clubs, and spades. In Spain and Portugal, it's sometimes swords, batons, coins, and cups.

You may also find cards that abbreviate the names of court cards in the language of the country—like R for King (*roi*), D for Queen (*dame*) and V for Jack (*valet*).

Other cards may have Russian, Arabic, or Chinese script. There are also funny decks, decks that advertise products, and decks of different sizes. All that variety can make for an interesting collection.

Cards are also fun to play at parties, whether it's with kids only or with aunts and uncles.

For every card game in the book, you will need a standard deck of 52 cards, unless stated otherwise.

Whatever you do with your cards or whatever you play, have fun!

Want a terrific tip? Harvard mathematicians say that seven ordinary shuffles are needed to guarantee that the cards are thoroughly mixed.

Now you know!

1
Card Games
for the
Very Young

Pig

This is a hilarious game for children or for adults to play with children. Anybody can learn it in two or three minutes, and one extra minute makes you an expert.

The Object of the Game

To get four of a kind in your own hand, or to be quick to notice it when somebody else gets four of a kind.

The Deal

Select from the deck four cards of a kind for each player in the game.

For example, five players would use twenty cards: four Aces, four Kings, four Queens, four Jacks, and four 10s. For six players you would add the 9s.

Any player shuffles and deals four cards to each player.

The Play

The players look at their cards to see if they were dealt four of a kind. If nobody has four of a kind, each player puts some unwanted card facedown on the table and passes it to the player to the left, receiving a card at the same time from the player to the right.

If still nobody has four of a kind, each player once again passes a card to the left and gets a new card from the right.

The game continues in this way until one player gets four of a kind. That player stops passing or receiving cards. Instead—she puts a finger to her nose!

The other players must be quick to notice this, and stop passing cards in order to put a finger to their nose. The last one to do it is the Pig.

Donkey

You play this game in the same way as "Pig," except that when you get four of a kind, you put your hand of cards facedown on the table quietly instead of putting your finger to your nose.

You still get a card from your right, but you just pass it along to your left, leaving your four of a kind untouched on the table.

As the other players see what has happened, they likewise put their cards down quietly. The idea is to keep up the passing and the conversation while some player plays on without realizing that the hand has really ended.

If you're the last player to put your cards on the table, you lose the hand. This makes you a D. The next time you lose, you become a D-O. The third time you become a D-O-N. This keeps on until finally you become a D-O-N-K-E-Y.

The D-O-N-K-E-Y loses the game, and the winner is the player who has the smallest number of letters.

Donkey Buttons

You need buttons for this game. It is the same as "Donkey," except that when you get four of a kind, you shout "Donkey!" and quickly grab a button from the middle of the table. There is one button less than there are players, so the last player to grab doesn't get a button, and becomes a D. The game continues in this way until somebody becomes a D-O-N-K-E-Y.

At the end of the game, the D-O-N-K-E-Y has to bray "Heehaw" three times.

My Ship Sails

The Object of the Game
To get seven cards of the same suit.

The Deal
Any player shuffles and deals seven cards to each player.

The Play
Each player looks at his hand and passes one card to the left, receiving at the same time one card from the right. The play goes on in the same way as in "Pig" or "Donkey." The only difference is that you are trying to collect cards that are all of the same suit, instead of four of a kind.

There are many different ways of ending a hand. When you get seven cards of the same suit, you put your cards down immediately and say, "My ship sails!"

Another way is to say nothing, but to put your finger to your nose as in "Pig."

If it takes too long to finish a hand, try one of the shorter games like "My Bee Buzzes" or "My Star Twinkles" (page 16).

My Star Twinkles

of players: 3–13

This is the same game as "My Ship Sails," except that you need only five cards of the same suit (and two odd cards) to win a hand. In this game, it takes only two or three minutes to play a hand.

My Bee Buzzes

of players: 3–13

This is the same game as "My Ship Sails," except that you need only six cards of the same suit to end the hand. Each player gets seven cards, but needs only six cards in the same suit (and one odd card) to win the hand. It takes less time to finish a hand in this game.

# of players: 3–13

The Object of the Game

To win the most cards.

The Deal

The dealer shuffles and deals four cards to each player.

The Play

The dealer begins by saying, "I looked through the window and saw. . . ." Just at this moment, and not before, he turns up one of his four cards, so that all the players can see it.

Then, each player—including the dealer—must try to say an animal or thing beginning with the same letter of the alphabet as the card that has been turned up.

For example, if the card is an Ace, you might call out, "Ant," "Alligator," "Alaska," or anything else

*that begins with the letter A. If the card is a 9,
you might call out "Nachos" or "Nut."*

The first player to call out a correct word
takes the card and starts his pile of captured
cards separate from the four cards that were
dealt to him.

Then the person to the left of the dealer says,
"I looked through the window and saw. . . ." and
turns up one of her cards.

The game continues in the same way, in turn
to the left, until all the cards originally dealt have
been turned up and captured. Each person keeps
his own pile of captured cards, and the one who
captures the most wins the game. The captured
cards have nothing to do with each player's original four cards, since each player had exactly four
chances to turn up a card.

When a word has been used to win a card, no
player can use that same word again.

For example, if you have used the word "Stone" to capture a 7, neither you nor any other player can use the word "Stone" to capture any other card beginning with an S.

Concentration

The Object of the Game
To capture the largest number of cards.

The Deal
Spread the cards facedown on a table. Don't bother to put them down neatly, but just jumble them up, making sure that no two cards overlap.

The Play
Before they begin, the players need to know what their turn is, whether they are first, second, third, and so on.

The first player turns up any card and then turns up any other card. If the two cards match (for example, if they are two Aces or two Kings), the first player captures them as her pair. She then gets another turn, and proceeds to turn up two more cards in the hope of finding a pair. When she turns up two cards that are not a pair, she must turn them facedown again in the same position. It now becomes the turn of the next player.

Tossing Cards into a Hat

# of players: any number

You need an old deck of cards for this game—or if you're playing with more than three people—two old decks. You also need an old felt or straw hat and a sheet of newspaper.

The Object of the Game
To toss the largest number of cards into the hat.

The Deal
Divide the cards equally among the players.

The Play
Place the hat on a sheet of newspaper at the other end of the room with its crown down and brim up.

Standing the whole length of the room away from the hat, each player in turn flips one card towards the hat, with the object of landing the card inside the hat.

Each player keeps track of the cards he has landed inside the hat. If a card lands on the brim, it counts as only one half a point. If a card on the brim of the hat is knocked in by any player, it counts a full point for the player who originally threw it.

Tip

The secret is to hold the card between your thumb and forefinger with your wrist bent inward toward your body. If you then straighten out your wrist suddenly with a flick and release the card at the same time, you can make it sail all the way across a very long room, and you can control it pretty well.

Although strength is not important in this game, small children may have trouble getting the knack.

Let them stand several paces closer to the hat.

Special Advice

Be sure to place the hat near a blank wall and far away from a piano or a sofa, or any other heavy piece of furniture. Cards that land under a piano are very hard to recover.

# of players: any number

You need two packs of cards for this hunt.

The Object of the Game
To be the first team to find all the hidden cards.

The Preparation
Before the players arrive, hide some of the cards from one of the decks in the room you are devoting to the game. Make sure to hide as many red cards as black ones.

People should be able to find a hidden card without having to move anything to get it. For example, if you hide a card in a bookcase, it should be sticking out in some way and not hidden inside any book. Every hidden card should be well within the reach of even the youngest child. It is perfectly fair to put a card under the pedals of a piano, but not on top of the piano, where a small child would be unable to see it.

Remove from the second deck cards that match the ones you have hidden.

The Play

When the players arrive, appoint two captains and let them choose sides. One team is to find red cards (Hearts and Diamonds), and the other team black cards (Spades and Clubs).

Give each player a card from the second deck and explain that she is to find a duplicate of it, hidden somewhere in a particular room or in two or three rooms, depending on how much space you have for the game. As soon as a player finds the card she is looking for, she is to bring it back to you and get a new card to look for. The team to find most of the hidden cards wins the game.

Tip

Be sure to explain that it isn't necessary to move anything in order to find the cards. Mention, also, that anybody who finds a card that he isn't looking for should replace it in exactly the same spot and tell no one about it. Somebody else will be looking for it, or he himself may be looking for it later on.

This is a good game to play in somebody else's house!

Slapjack

"Slapjack" is one of the most entertaining games that you can play with a deck of cards.

The Object of the Game
To win all the cards.

The Deal
Deal one card at a time to each player until all the cards are dealt. It doesn't matter if they don't come out even. The players square up their cards into a neat pile facedown in front of them without looking at any of the cards.

The Play
The player to the left of the dealer begins by lifting the top card of her pile and dropping it face-up in the middle of the table. The next player (to the left of the first) does the same—lifts the top

card of his pile and drops it faceup in the middle of the table on top of the card that is already there.

The game continues in this way—until any player turns up a Jack. Then the fun begins. The first player to slap that Jack wins the entire pile of cards in the middle of the table! If more than one player slaps the Jack, the one whose hand is at the bottom wins the pile.

This means that you have to keep your eyes open and be pretty quick to get your hand down on a Jack. Sometimes another player slaps your hand instead of the Jack, but it's all in fun.

I used to beat my grandfather because he would lift his hand high in the air before bringing it down on a Jack, while I would swoop in sideways and snatch the Jack away before his hand hit the table. Grandpa never seemed to learn!

When you win cards, put them facedown underneath the cards you already have.

The play goes on until one player has won all

the cards. As soon as a player has lost his last card, he may watch for the next Jack and try to slap it in order to get a new pile for himself. If he fails to get that next pile, he is out of the game. Sooner or later, all the players except one are "knocked out," and the cards all come to one player, who is the winner.

False Slaps

A player who slaps at a card that is *not* a Jack must give the top card of her pile to the owner of the card that she slapped. If the false slapper has no cards to pay the penalty, she is out.

How to Turn Cards

At your turn to play, you must lift the top card of your pile and turn it away from you as you drop it faceup in the middle of the table. This is to make sure that you don't see the card before the other players do. Also, make sure that you let the card go as you drop it. Naturally, you don't want the other players to have a big advantage, so turn the card over very quickly. Then you will see it just about as soon as they do.

Tip

Most players use the same hand for turning the cards and for slapping at Jacks. It's a more exciting game, however, if you agree that the hand used for slapping will not be the same hand used for turning the cards.

Some players use the right hand to turn over the card with a quick motion, and they swoop down on the Jack with the left hand.

You may want to try it both ways to see which is better for you.

The important thing to remember is that it's better to be a swift swooper than a slow slapper.

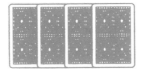

# of players: 3–8

The Object of the Game

To win all the cards.

The Deal

Any player deals one card at a time until all the cards have been dealt. They don't have to come out even.

The Play

As in "Slapjack," each player turns up one card at a time at his turn to play. The card must be turned away from the player and dropped on the table, except that each player starts a pile in front of himself for his turned up cards.

For example, in a game of four players, after each player has had a turn, there will be four piles of faceup cards, and four piles of cards facedown that were dealt at the beginning.

When a player turns up a card that matches a faceup card on any other pile, the first player to say "Snap!" wins both piles and puts them face down under her own facedown pile.

A player who says "Snap" at the wrong time, when the turned-up card does not match one of the other piles, must give the top card of his pile to the player who just turned up her card.

As in "Slapjack," a player who runs out of cards may stay in for the next "Snap" in hopes of getting a new pile. If she does not win that "Snap," she is out. A player who cries a false "Snap" is out if he has no cards to pay the penalty.

Special Rule

My grandmother used to play this game with me. She preferred it to "Slapjack," which can become rough. We had to make a special rule once because one little girl who was playing with us said "Snap!" every time a card was turned. She had to pay a penalty card most of the time, but this was more than offset because she won every single pile. Grandma said this wasn't fair, so we adopted the rule that after three false "Snaps" a player was out.

Tip

Keep looking around to make sure you know which cards are on top of the piles, since these keep changing as the game goes on. You need to be ready at all times to shout "Snap!" very quickly. If two or more players begin the word at the same time, the player who ends the word first wins. If you're a slow talker, this is no game for you.

# of players: 4

The Object of the Game

To get four cards of the same value (four 4's, or four Queens, etc.) and announce it before your opponents discover it.

The Deal

Game is for two sets of partners (4 players). Partners sit across from each other. The dealer gives four cards to each player and then puts four cards faceup in a row on the table.

The Play

As soon as the dealer says "Go," players may exchange a card in their hand for a card on the table—as many times as they like (continuing with cards that other players lay down). Players usually make several exchanges so that their opponents will not guess what cards they are collecting). When the flurry of exchanges stops, dealer says "Flush," removes the cards on the table, and deals out four new ones, so that the exchanges can begin again. When your partner judges that you have four cards of the same rank, she says "Kent," and you show your hand. If she is right, you and your partner win that hand. If one of your opponents judges that you have four of a kind, he says, "Stop," and if he was right you lose the hand; if he was wrong you win.

What makes this game special
Unlike most card games with partners, you are allowed to tell your partner what you have through a code you work out between you—any kind of code—words, hand signals, whatever—to

tell when you have Kent (four of a kind). Opponents will try to figure out the code, so you have to be tricky. You can give your signals only during the time between "Go" and "Flush."

Scoring

Decide on a number and the first team to win that many games is the winning team.

Codes

Here are some ideas for codes:

If you name a fruit, it means you have Kent; a vegetable means you're bluffing. (Say lots of vegetable names to confuse the other team).

Everything you say will be true if your baseball cap is turned backwards; otherwise, false.

Subtract one for every number you use. If you say "I have five 3s," it means you have four 2s.

If you scratch your head it means you have Kent. Your partner is to ignore all other movements you make. (And you make lots of movements to confuse your opponents).

2
The War Family

War

The Object of the Game
To win all the cards.

The Deal
Deal one card to each player until the deck is divided in two.

The Play
The players put their stack of cards facedown in front of them and turn up the top card at the same time. The player who has the higher of the two turned-up cards wins both cards and puts them facedown at the bottom of his stack of cards. The King is the highest card, and the Ace is the lowest. The full rank of cards is:

Sometimes "War" is played with the Ace high.

If the two turned-up cards are of the same rank, the players have a "war." Each turns one card facedown and one card faceup. The higher of the two new faceup cards takes both piles (a total of six cards).

If the newly turned-up cards again match, there is *double war.* Each player once again turns one card facedown and one card faceup, and the higher of these two new faceup cards wins the entire pile of ten cards.

The game continues until one player has all the cards.

This is a good game to play when you have a lot of time and nowhere to go.

War for Three

The Object of the Game

To win all the cards.

The Deal

When three players want to play "War," take one card out of the deck and give seventeen cards to each.

The Play

The play is much the same as in two-handed "War," but when two cards turned up are the same, all three players join in the war by turning one card facedown and one card face up. If two of the new turned up cards are the same, all three players must once more turn one card facedown and one card faceup. As usual, the highest card wins all cards that are used in the war.

If all three turned up cards are the same, the

players must engage in double war. Each player turns two cards facedown and one card faceup. If the result is a tie, all three players engage in single war.

The Persian Card Game

This simple card game is a good one for two beginners or for a child to play with an adult.

The Object of the Game
To capture all the cards in the deck.

The Deal
Divide the cards equally between the players. They rank from Ace down to 2, which is low.

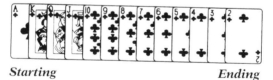

Starting   **Ending**

The Play
Players turn the top card of their piles faceup on the table at the same time. If they turn up cards

of different suits, nothing happens and they turn up the next cards. They continue doing this until they simultaneously turn up cards of the same *suit*—such as two Hearts, two Diamonds, two Spades, or two Clubs. When that happens, the player with the higher card wins all the cards the other player has turned up. These go at the bottom of his or her pack.

Sometimes you may go completely through the deck once or twice without turning up cards of the same suit. In that case, the game is over and the one with the larger number of cards is the winner.

Revenge

The Object of the Game

To get rid of all your cards by putting them onto the other player's pack. You do it by coming up with a card that is one rank higher—or lower—than the card your opponent has just turned up.

The Deal

Divide the pack, card by card.

The Play

Let's say your opponent starts the game by turning over the top card in his pile and it's a 6 of Hearts. If you turn up a 7 of any suit, you can place it on your opponent's 6. You get another turn. Suppose the next card you turn up is an 8. Over it goes—onto your opponent's pack, and you get another turn.

You can build down too. If the next card you get is another 7, you can place that on the 8 you just put down. If you cannot place the next card on your opponent's pack, your turn ends.

Gradually, as you play, you build up long sequences of cards that follow each other in order. Eventually, when you get the chance to put a card on your opponent's pile, you don't put on just one—you put on 15 or 20 or more! This is what makes the game such fun. Your opponent can be within two cards of winning when you suddenly zap him with almost the whole deck— now that's revenge!

When you have gone through your pile of cards, turn them over and start again. The game goes on until one player is out of cards.

Tip

You can give your opponent cards from the top of your deck or from your discard pile, but be careful. If you're in the middle of a sequence, you don't want to break it by taking a single card from the discard deck. Then again, that one card from the discard pile may lead to an even longer run.

Pishe Pasha

Pronounced PISH-uh PAY-sha, this game is played the same way as "Revenge" but with one added element. Whenever an Ace comes up, it is put out in the middle of the table and built upon. And there is no choice about putting cards up in the middle. Even if you are in the middle of a steady run of cards, you must interrupt it to play a card to the middle, building in suits, when it belongs there. Often, two decks are used for this game.

# of players: 2

The Object of the Game

To be the first to get rid of all your cards and score 50 or 100 points, whichever you decide on before the game starts.

The Deal

Get rid of all the 2s, 3s, 4s, 5s, and 6s from the deck. You will be playing with the 32 remaining cards, which rank from the 7, which is low, to the Ace, which is high.

Deal eight cards to each player and place the rest facedown in a pile on the table.

The Play

The first player, let's call him Frank, starts by placing a card from his hand faceup on the table. The other player, Gale, must turn up a card of the same suit if she can. She then sets those two cards aside, out of play. The one who played the higher ranking card now plays the next card—any card at all—as long as it is of a different suit from the previous one.

If Frank cannot match Gale's card, he must take a card from the pile on the table and add it to his hand. Then it is his turn to play.

When the game comes to a standstill, and neither player can come up with a card to match the other, the round is over, and you count up the score.

Scoring

Score one point for each card remaining in your opponent's hand. The first person to get a score or 50 or 100 points, depending on how long you want to play, wins.

The Object of the Game

To win all the cards.

The Deal

Give each player half the deck.

The Play

The non-dealer puts a card faceup in the middle of the table. If it is an ordinary spot card (2-10), the dealer covers it with a card from the top of his pile. This process continues, each playing one card in turn on top of the pile, until one of the players puts down an Ace, King, Queen, or Jack.

The moment an Ace or picture card appears, the other player must pay out the proper number of cards, one at a time, faceup:

For an Ace, four cards.
For a King, three cards.
For a Queen, two cards.
For a Jack, one card.

If all the cards put down in payment are spot cards, the owner of the Ace or picture card takes up the entire pile and puts it at the bottom of his stack. This is the way cards are won, and the object of the game is to win all of them.

If, however, you turn up an Ace or picture card while you are paying your opponent, the payment stops and he must now pay you for the card that you have put down.

The game continues, since either player may turn up an Ace or picture card while making a payment. Eventually, however, a player turns up only spot cards in payment, and then the entire pile is lost.

The Object of the Game

To win all the cards.

The Deal

Deal one card at a time to each player until the entire deck has been dealt. It makes no difference if the cards don't come out even.

The Play

Each player takes the name of an animal, such as Pig, Kangaroo, Rhinoceros, Hippopotamus.

When everybody fully understands which player represents which animal, the play begins. The player to the dealer's left turns up a card and then each player in turn turns up a card. As in "Snap," the action takes place when a card that has just been turned up matches some other card that is faceup on somebody's pile.

The players who own the matching cards must each call out the animal that the other represents. The first to say the other's animal name three times wins both piles.

For example, suppose three players, George, Pat, and Ed, have adopted the names Goat, Pig, and Elephant. George turns up a Queen. Pat turns up a 10, and Ed turns up a Queen. George and Ed go into action, but the Pat must keep silent. George shouts, "Elephant, Elephant, Elephant!" And Ed shouts, "Goat, Goat, Goat!" Both piles are won by the player who finishes talking first.

Play continues until one player has all the cards.

Tip

As you may have noticed, it takes longer to say, "Elephant, Elephant, Elephant!" than it does to say, "Goat, Goat, Goat!" For this reason, it always pays to give yourself a long animal name rather than a short one. The longer it takes your opponent to say it three times, the better for you!

Good names to use are hippopotamus, rhinoceros, elephant, mountain lion, boa constrictor, and orangutan.

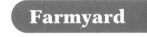

Farmyard

# of players: 3 or more

This is the same game as "Animals," except that the players go by the noises made by a few farmyard animals instead of their names.

For example, a player who chose Cow would be called "Moo-Moo-Moo," rather than "Cow-Cow-Cow." A player who chose a Duck would be called "Quack-Quack-Quack," ad a player who chose Cat would be called "Meow-Meow-Meow," and so on.

I Doubt It

When you have three or four players, use one deck of cards. When you are playing with five or more, shuffle two packs together.

The Object of the Game
To get rid of all your cards.

The Deal
Two or three cards at a time are dealt so that each player gets an equal number of cards. When only a few cards are left, deal one at a time as far as the cards will go.

The Play
The player to the dealer's left puts from one to four cards facedown in the middle of the table, announcing that she is putting down that number of Aces.

The next player puts down one to four cards and announces that he is putting down that number of 2s.

The next player in turn does the same thing, stating that he is putting down that number of 3s. And the play proceeds in this sequence:

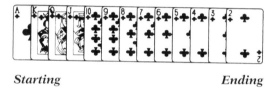

Starting   **Ending**

When any player puts down cards and makes his announcement, any other player may say, "I doubt it." The suspect cards must immediately be turned faceup. If the statement was true, the doubter must take the entire pile into his hand. If the statement was false, the player who made the false statement must take the pile.

When you're using two packs shuffled together, a player may put down any number of cards, from one to eight.

When a player puts his last cards n the table, some other player must say, "I doubt it," since otherwise the game ends automatically. If the statement turns out to be true, the player wins the game.

A player who has no cards at all of the kind that she is supposed to put down is not allowed to skip her turn. She must put down one or more cards anyway and try to get away with her untruthful announcement. If somebody doubts her claim, she will have to pick up the pile.

If two or more people say, "I doubt it," at the same time, the one nearest the player's left wins the tie and must pick up the pile, if the statement turns out to be true after all.

Three Card "I Doubt It"

The Deal

The cards are dealt out equally as far as they will go. Put any remaining cards face down in the middle of the table.

The Play

Each player in turn puts down exactly three cards. Instead of starting with Aces automatically, the first player may choose any denomination.

For example, she may say, "Three 9s." The next player must say, "Three 10s," and so on.

When a player has one or two cards left, he must draw enough cards from those put facedown in the middle of the table to make up the three he needs.

3

Games with a Mathematical Twist

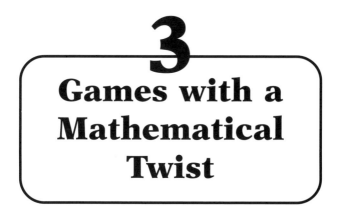

Plus or Minus One

The Object of the Game

To build all the cards into a single pile.

Point Value of the Cards

Hold the deck facedown and deal the top card faceup to the table to start the "build." Turn up cards one at a time. If the turned-up card is one less or one greater than the faceup card, put it on top. If not, put it in a discard pile.

For example: If the faceup card is an 8 of spades, you can put either a 7 or a 9 of any suit on it. You can put a King on an Ace, and an Ace on a King.

Continue playing until all the cards are dealt out. Then turn over the discard pile and go on playing. For a tougher game: Allow only two deals of the discard pile.

Interesting Twist

When you win a game, count the number of times you had to go through the deck. When you lose, count how many cards are left in the discard pile. That way some wins are better than others—and some losers aren't so bad!

Plus or Minus Two

This is played exactly like "Plus or Minus One," except that instead of putting down a card that is one less or one more of the faceup card, you put down a card that is two less or two more.

Sevens

The Object of the Game

To get rid of all the cards.

Point Value of the Cards

    Ace = 1

    Jack = 11

    Queen = 12

    King = 13

Play

Deal cards in a row, faceup. Remove all sevens and all cards that are next to each other that add up to seven or any multiple of seven.

For example, a King, worth 13, and an 8 side by side, add up to 21 [3 x 7] and therefore can be removed.

The Object of the Game
To get rid of all the cards.

The Layout
Deal nine faceup cards in three rows of three.

Play
Cover—with faceup cards from the pack—any two cards that total 9. Cover any single nines. Cover the 10, Jack, Queen, and King whenever two of the same suit are exposed. Continue covering cards until there are no more cards that can be covered—in which case the game is lost—or until the entire deck is laid out.

Then pick up the piles that would normally get covered—pairs where the top cards total 9, a pile with a 9 on the top, two piles with any same suit 10, Jack, Queen, or King. If no piles remain, you've won.

Knuckles

This game got its name because a player can rap the table with his knuckles at any time during the game if he thinks he has the lower score. Both players show their hands, and the one with the lower score wins.

The Object of the Game
To end up with the cards totaling the lowest possible score.

Point Value of the Cards
Cards from 2 to 10 = face value.
Ace = 1 point
Jack = 0 points
Queen and King = 10 points each

The Deal
The dealer deals out five cards to each player and

places the rest of the deck facedown in the middle of the table.

The Play

The first player takes the top card of the pack and may exchange it for any card in his hand. He makes this exchange only if the new card is lower than one of the cards in his hand. The discarded card is played faceup beside the facedown pack. The next player may take the faceup card or pick the top card of the pack and either change it for a card in her hand or discard it.

Play continues, with players changing cards in their hands for lower ones, until all the cards in the pack have been picked. The player with the lowest cards is the winner. The winner is, invariably, the one with the most Jacks and Aces.

Finders Keepers

The Object of the Game

To take in cards that add up to an amount you've decided ahead of time.

Point Value of the Cards

Ace = 1 point
2-10 = face value
Jack = 11 points
Queen = 12 points
King = 13 points

The Deal

Lay out all the cards facedown in six rows of eight cards, with a seventh row of four cards.

The Play

Player #1 names a number and then turns up any two cards. If the cards total that number, he takes in both cards. If not, he leaves one card faceup and turns the other over again in its original place.

Player #2 then turns up two cards to see if she can find cards that make up the number. If she is successful, she takes in the cards. If not, she leaves one faceup and turns over the other.

When a player succeeds in making the total, she chooses the next number that will be the sum the players try to make.

The winner is the one who has the most cards when all the cards have been turned up.

Hit the Mark

The Object of the Game
To have cards totalling the lowest value.

The Deal
Deal five facedown cards to each player. Put the rest of the deck in the center of the table.

The Play
Players take turns turning up cards from the center pile. At your turn, you may trade one of your facedown cards for a faceup card, immediately turning the new card facedown in its place. Add the discarded card to the faceup pile. It may be taken by an opponent, if she wants to make a trade.

At any point in the game, a player who thinks his cards have a low total value may "knock." By knocking on the table, he announces that he wants to turn his cards face up. All players then do so. The winner is the player whose cards have the lowest total value.

Point Value of the Cards

Ace = 1 point
2-10 = face value
King and Queen = 10 points each
Jack = 0 points

Mark's Place

The Object of the Game

To get the highest value four-digit number in a special sequence. In the thousands place (to the left), you have to have a spade; in the hundreds place (second from left) you need a Heart; in the tens place (third from the left), you need a Diamond, and in the ones place (on the right), you need a Club.

The Deal

Remove all the face cards from the deck. You'll have 40 cards left.

Deal four facedown cards to each player. Place the remainder of the deck in the center of the table and turn up the top card.

Point Value of the Cards

Spades = Thousands (for instance, 5 of
Spades would be 5,000 points)

Hearts = Hundreds (for instance, 2 of Hearts
would be 200 points)

Diamonds = Tens (7 of Diamonds would
be 70)

Clubs = Ones (9 of Clubs would be 9)

The Play

The player to the dealer's left may take the
turned-up card and exchange it for one of his
cards. When he discards, he turns the card he
doesn't want faceup and places it next to the deck
to form a discard pile. If he does not want the
faceup card, he takes the top card and can either

exchange it for one of his cards or discard it.

Play continues to the left, with each player having the option of taking the top faceup card on the discard pile or the top card of the pack.

As soon as a player thinks he has a card of each suit in the correct place, and believes he has constructed the highest four-digit number of the group, he can "knock"—demand that all players turn up their cards and compare them.

Scoring

If the player who knocked does have the highest value, he gets from each of the others the difference between his number and the highest value the player can construct. If a player doesn't have the required suit in its place, it counts as a zero.

For example, if a player's turned-up cards are the 3 of Hearts, the 7 of Hearts, the 2 of Diamonds, and the 6 of Diamonds, his number would be:

0720 or 720

If he has the 2 of Spades, the 5 of Hearts, the 4 of Clubs, and the 8 of Clubs, his number would be:

2508

If a player has a higher number than the player who knocked, he gets double the value of the difference between his number and the knocker's number. Plus, he gets from the others the difference between his number and theirs.

The first player whose score totals 10,000 is the winner.

Add and Subtract

The Object of the Game

To be the first to get the desired total—70 for the "Add" player, and 30 for the "Subtract" player.

The Deal

Both players pick a card to decide which one will be "Add" and which one "Subtract." The player with the higher card is "Add." Deal out the entire deck so that each player has half the deck in a facedown pile in front of him.

Point Value of the Cards

All cards = face value

Jack = 11 points

Queen = 12 points

King = 13 points

The Play

Start out with 50 points. The two players take turns placing their top cards on a pile in the middle of the table, adding or subtracting the card's value from the total.

Here is a sample of what might happen—Adam is "Add" and Sally is "Subtract."

Adam plays a 7: 50 + 7 = 57
Sally plays a 9: 57 – 9 = 48
Adam plays a 3: 48 + 3 = 51
Sally plays a King: 51 – 13 = 38   and so on.

Scoring

If the total reaches 70 exactly, the Add player is the winner. If it falls to 30 exactly, Subtract is the winner. If the cards run out before there is a winner, reshuffle them, turn them over, and go on playing.

Zero

The Object of the Game
To win all the cards.

The Deal
Divide the cards between the two players.

Point Value of the Cards
Cards = face value
Ace = 1
Jack = 11
Queen = 12
King = 13

Black cards are added (+)
Red cards are subtracted (−)

The Play
Both players turn up cards at the same time, like in "War," but they turn up two at a time instead

of one. The player whose total value is closest to zero (0) takes all four cards and puts them in a facedown pile.

For example, if Josh has the 4 of Spades and the Queen of Diamonds (+4 and –12 = –8), and Sandy has the 4 of Diamonds and the King of Clubs (–4 and +13 = + 9), then Josh is the winner.

In case there's a tie, each player turns up two more cards and totals them. The winner of that trick takes in all eight cards.

4
The Authors Family

Go Fish

# of players: 3–5

The Object of the Game

To form more "books" than any other player. A book in this game is four of a kind, such as four Kings, four Queens, and so on.

The Deal

If only two play, deal seven cards to each. If four or five play, deal five cards to each. Put the rest of the pack facedown on the table, forming the stock.

The Play

The player to the dealer's left begins. Let's say that's you. You say to some other player, "Jane, give me your 9s." You must mention the name of the player you are speaking to (Jane), and you must mention the exact rank that you want (9s), and you must have at least one card of the rank that you are asking for (9) in your hand.

The player you are speaking to (Jane), must hand over all the 9s she has in her hand, but if she has none, she says, "Go Fish."

Then you draw the top card of the stock. The turn to ask then passes to the player to your left.

If you succeed in getting some cards when you ask for them, you keep your turn and may ask again. You may ask the same player or some different player, and you may ask for any rank in your new question.

If you have been told to "go fish" and you pick a card of the rank you just asked for, you show the card immediately before putting it in your hand, and your turn continues. (In some very strict games, your turn would continue only if the

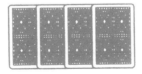

card you fished for completed a book for you.)

When you get the fourth card of a book, you show all four, place them on the table in front of you, and continue your turn.

If a player is left without cards, she may draw from the stock at her turn and ask for cards of the same rank as the one she has drawn. After the stock has been used up, a player who has no cards is out of the game.

The game is over when all 13 books have been assembled. The player with the most books wins.

Tips

When a player asks for cards and gets them, but does not put down a completed book, you can tell that he has either two or three cards of that rank.

Suppose John requests Queens and gets one Queen from the player he has asked. John does not put down a book of Queens, but asks some new question and is told to "go fish." You now know that John held at least one Queen to give him the right to ask for Queens. He has received a Queen, which gives him a total of either two or three Queens.

In the same way, you know something else about a player's hand when he asks for a card and gets nothing at all.

For example, suppose John asks somebody for 8s and is told to go fish. You know that he must have at least one 8 in his hand.

Little by little, you can build up information about the cards the other players are holding. If you know that another player has Queens, but you have no Queens yourself, the information does you no good. If you have a Queen yourself, however, you are then allowed to ask for Queens—and if you ask the right person because of the information you have, you may get as many as three Queens and be able to put down an entire book in front of you!

Fish for Minnows

This is a simpler way of playing "Go Fish," and it is especially good for very young players.

The Object of the Game

To get the most pairs.

The Deal

Deal out all the cards, not worrying about it if they don't happen to come out even.

The Play

At your turn, you ask for a rank, and the player who has been asked must hand over one such card, if she has one. The object is to form pairs instead of books of four. As soon as you get a pair, you put it face down in front of you.

Authors

This game is a lot like "Go Fish," but it can be played with great skill.

The Object of the Game
To win more books (4 cards of the same rank) than any other player.

The Deal
Deal out all 52 cards, even though they may not come out even.

The Play
At your turn, you ask for a single card naming both its rank and its suit. For example, you might say, "Bill, give me the Jack of Spades." Your turn continues if you get the card you asked for, but it passes to the left as soon as you ask for a card that the player doesn't have.

You can buy decks of cards that are specially made for playing "Authors," so that you can ask a player for William Shakespeare or Ernest Hemingway. But it's just as much fun to play "Authors" with a regular deck of cards.

Old Maid or Odd One Out

The Object of the Game

To avoid getting "stuck" with the last unpaired Queen.

The Deal

Discard one Queen from the pack before beginning this game. Deal one card at a time to each player, as far as the cards will go. It doesn't matter if they don't come out even.

The Play

Sort your cards and put aside, facedown, all cards that you can pair—two by two. For example, you might put aside two Kings, two Queens, two 7s, and so on. If you have three Queens and three Jacks, you would be allowed to put two of them aside, but the third card would stay in your hand.

After each player has discarded his paired cards, the dealer presents her cards, fanned out, but facedown, to the player at her left. The player at the left selects one card (blindly, since the hand is facedown) and quickly examines it to see if it pairs with some card still in his hand. If so, he discards the pair. In any case, this player now fans his cards out and presents them face down to the player at his left.

This game continues, each player in turn presenting his hand, fanned out and facedown, to the player to the left. Eventually, every card will be paired, except one of the Queens. The player who is left with the odd Queen at the end of the hand is the "Old Maid" or the "Odd One Out."

Whenever a player's last card is taken, he drops out. He can no longer be the "Old Maid" or the "Odd One Out."

5
Card Games from Many Countries

Scopa

This is an Italian game. Scopa means "broom."

The Object of the Game
The first player to get 11 points is the winner.

The Deal
Remove the 8s, 9s, and 10s from the deck.
The dealer deals four cards to each player and four faceup cards on the table.

Point Value of the Cards
All number cards equal their face value.
Jack = 8 points
Queen = 9 points
King = 10 points

The Play
Players take turns playing a card from their

hands. A card may be used as a "match" to take in a card of the same value. Or it can take in more than one card, if the card to be played equals the total of two or more cards on the table.

For example, a 6 and a 2 on the table may be taken by a Jack (which is worth 8 points). A 3 and an Ace could be taken by a 4.

When you take in cards, keep them facedown in a pile in front of you.

If you manage at any point to pick up the last card on the table, that is a "scopa." Turn that card up in the pile of accumulated cards, to be scored separately when you tally your points.

After the four cards have been played out, the dealer deals four more to each player. The play continues until all the cards have been dealt. Then players tally their points.

Scoring

Each turned up card (scopa) = 1 point

Each seven = 1 point

King of Diamonds = 1 point

The most cards = 1 point

The most Diamonds = 1 point

# of players: 3

This French game is called "Marriage," which actually means the wedding ceremony.

The Object of the Game
To avoid being the one holding the key card at the end.

The Deal
The dealer chooses the key card and removes the same color card of that value from the deck. For example, if she chooses the 5 of Diamonds, she removes the 5 of Hearts from the deck. But she doesn't let the other players know what card she has chosen. She deals out the entire deck.

The Play
Players remove from their hands pairs of cards of

the same color and value—for example, the 4 of Spades and the 4 of Clubs.

When all pairs have been removed, each player in turn may pick a card from the hand of the player to his right. As the same color pairs are formed, they are removed from the person's hand. The player left with the key card is the loser.

# of players: 2–6

There seems to be some version of "Crazy Eights" in every part of the world. This version comes from Brisbane, Australia.

The Object of the Game
To be the first to get rid of all your cards.

Point Value of the Cards
Cards equal face value, face cards count 10 points each.

The Deal
Deal eight cards to each player. Place the rest of the deck facedown in the middle of the table. Turn up the top card of the deck and place it beside the deck.

The Play
The players in turn must play a card to the

turned-up card. It may be a card of the same suit or rank as the top card. However, if a player puts down an Ace, he can switch the action to any suit he wants.

Shuffle, deal the cards again, and go on playing until one player's score reaches a number you've decided on ahead of time—like 100 points. That player is the loser.

The first player to get rid of all her cards is the winner of the hand. Cards left in the losers' hands are added up and count against them.

# of players: 2

This Greek game has echoes of "Casino," which you'll find later in this book.

The Object of the Game

To earn points by taking in key cards.

Point Value of the Cards

Cards are not ranked in play, but Jacks are "wild" (meaning they can take on any value), so they can be used as a match for any card.

Jack, Queen, King, Ace = 1 point each

Ten of Diamonds = 2 points

Two of Clubs = 2 points

Each Xeri = 10 points

The Deal

Deal six cards to each player and four overlapping faceup cards on the table.

The Play

The non-dealer goes first. Players take turns playing a card from their hand to the top card of the faceup group. If the player has a card in hand of the same value as the card on the top, or has a Jack, the player takes in that card. Cards that are taken in are kept in a facedown stack in front of the player.

When only one card is left on the table, and a player takes it in, it is turned faceup in the player's stack as a "xeri." Each xeri counts as 10 points.

After the six cards have been played, six more are dealt. Play continues until all cards are dealt and played. Then players total their scores.

The game continues, alternating dealers, until one player has 100 points and is the winner.

# of players: 2 to 8

You need a token of some kind—a coin, pebble, dried bean, nut, etc.

The Object of the Game

To take the token that you put on the King and to be the first to get rid of your cards.

The Deal

Put four Kings in the middle. Players choose one of the kings to be the key card. Each player puts a token on that King, and one token in the middle.

Deal out the whole pack, creating one extra hand. If the dealer doesn't like his own hand, he can exchange it for the spare hand. If he doesn't want the spare hand, the next player may buy it, paying the dealer one token.

The Play

Whoever has the Ace of Spades plays first and must play that card. Or if there is no Ace of Spades, then the player who has the lowest spade plays it. The player who has the next card in that suit plays next. If no one can play, because the next card is not available, the one who played the last card must play the lowest red card in his hand.

Players follow suit in sequence until that suit is blocked and the next player to play a card must play her lowest black card.

The player who plays the Queen of the same suit as the chosen King (the one with the token on it) takes the token.

The first player to get rid of all his cards is the winner and takes all the tokens in the middle. If the token on the King is not claimed, it stays for the next round.

# of players: 2

The Object of the Game

To get rid of all the cards in your hand by playing them onto the layout.

The Deal

Remove the four Kings from the deck and lay them faceup to form four diagonal corners in a layout that will have four more faceup cards.

Deal four faceup cards, placing each between two Kings, to form the layout.

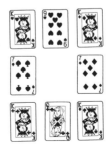

Deal eight cards to each player. Place the deck facedown in the middle of the table.

The Play

Players take turns. At each turn a player draws a card from the top of the deck and may play it onto the layout if it is opposite in color and one lower in value than one of the layout cards.

For example, you could play a red nine on a black ten, and a black Queen on a red King.

During her turn, a player may make all possible plays. If any of the cards in the layout itself can be placed on another, she may do it in her turn, filling the empty space with a card from her hand. Play continues until one player has no more cards and is the winner.

# of players: 2

This game originated in Quebec. It is the one of the only truly Canadian card games.

The Object of the Game
To win the most goals in three periods. A period consists of all the hands played in one deck.

The Deal
The dealer decides the number of cards she will deal in each hand and deals that number to herself and to her opponent.

The Play
Player #1 plays a card faceup to the center of the table. Player #2 partially covers it with a faceup card from his hand. If the card is of the same value—say a 2 on a 2—it is a "pass."

Two passes on two consecutive turns counts as a goal.

For example, if Sally plays a 3 and Tom follows with a 3, that is a pass. If Sally then plays another 3, she scores a goal. However, if Tom plays the fourth 3, it doesn't count.

A Jack is an automatic pass. If you play a Jack on a Jack that has just been played, you score a goal. This can be canceled by a third Jack. But the fourth Jack played can get the goal back.

When the cards are played out, the dealer deals another hand from the remaining cards until the deck is finished. This marks the end of the first period.

The deal changes hands for the second period, and then changes back for the third. If the score is tied at the end of three periods, the game goes into sudden-death overtime; the first player to score wins.

# of players: 2 or more

This game comes from Barbados. It is a variation on "Donkey."

The Object of the Game
To be the first to get rid of your cards.

The Deal
Players decide on the penalty for each card remaining in the loser's hand. These could be household chores, or silly acts to perform.

Deal three or four cards to each player. Put the pack facedown in the middle. Turn up the top card and place it beside the pack. This determines the suit to be played.

The Play
The first player must put down a card of the same suit as the turned-up card. If he can't play a card

of that suit, he "goes to pack"—the pack on the table—picking up cards, one at a time until he can play. Other players do the same. The player who played the highest card in the round takes in the whole pile and makes the next play. The card he plays determines the suit of the next round. The play continues until there are no more cards in the pack.

When this happens, the player picks up the last card put down, and one of his opponents must give him another card to play.

The first player to get rid of all his cards is the winner. The number of cards remaining in the loser's hand determines how many penalties he pays.

Tip

Try to play high cards so you can be the one to decide what suit is played.

Ace Frime

This game from France is one of many versions of rummy. In this type, the wild card changes from one hand to the next. *Frime* means "showing off."

The Object of the Game
To be first to get rid of all your cards.

The Deal
Deal seven cards to each player and put the rest of the deck in the center of the table. Turn up the top card and place it beside the deck.

The Play
The player to the left of the dealer takes a card (the turned-up card if he wants it, otherwise the top card of the pack) and discards one. Play continues to the left. At your turn, you may meld (lay

down sets or sequences of cards faceup in front of you) three or more cards of the same value or runs of three or more cards of the same suit in sequence.

You can—at your turn—add to any of the melds on the table. Turn the four cards over when you add the fourth member of a set.

When you put down your cards, the other players count the value of the cards in their hands. It counts against them.

The winner is the player with the lowest score after whatever number of hands you decide to play.

Point Value of the Cards

Ace through 10 = the card's face value. Ace counts as 1.

Jack, Queen, King = 10 points each

Wild card = 15 points.

Aces are wild in the first hand, two's in the second, then threes, and so on.

6
The
Stops Family

Sequence

This game has no "stops" at all, but it belongs in the family as a sort of great-grandfather of the other games. It is great for very young children.

The Object of the Game

To get rid of all your cards.

The Deal

Deal out one card at a time to each player until the deck is used up. It doesn't matter if some of the players are dealt more cards than the others.

The Play

The player to the dealer's left puts down his lowest card in any suit he chooses.

After the first card has been put on the table, whoever has the next highest card in the same suit must put it down. This continues until somebody finally plays the Ace of that suit.

The rank of the cards is:

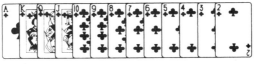

Highest   **Lowest**

For example, suppose that the first player's lowest Spade is the 4. He puts it down on the table. Somebody else plays the 5 of Spades, and another player puts down both the 6 and 7 of Spades (it doesn't matter if the same person plays two or more cards in a turn).

When the Ace is reached, the one who plays it must begin a new suit. As before, the player who begins the suit must begin with her lowest card in that suit.

Sooner or later, one of the players will get rid of all his cards. He wins the hand, and the other players lose one point for every card they still have when the hand comes to an end.

To make it simpler, you may want to forget about scoring and just play to win the hand.

Tip

Practically no skill is needed for this game. It is wise, though, to begin with the 2 of some suit when it is your turn to begin a play. If you have no 2, begin with a 3, or with the lowest card of any suit in your hand. If you don't follow this policy, you may eventually get stuck with a 2 or a 3 in your hand.

If very young players are playing, you might remove the picture cards from the deck and use only the cards from Ace to 10. Then, of course, Ace is the lowest and 10 is the highest card of each suit.

# of players: 2 or more

This game is also known as "Drop 7" and "Fan-Tan."

The Object of the Game
To get rid of all your cards.

The Deal
All the cards are dealt out.

The Play
Each player is allowed to play one card. The player to the dealer's right goes first, then each player in turn. To begin, the player must have the 7 of Diamonds, so the player has to pass if he cannot put down that card. The player who has it places it on the table.

Players in turn may play the 7 of Clubs or the 6 or 8 of Diamonds, placing the 6 on one side of the 7 and the 8 on the other side.

The next players may continue to place cards in sequence, building up (on the 8) or down (on the 6), or they may play a 7. But you can only play the suits in order. The 7 of Hearts may be played only after the 7 of Clubs has been played, and the 7 of Spades only after the 7 of Hearts.

Players must play a card if they have a play. Otherwise, they pass. Play continues until one player gets rid of all his cards and is the winner.

Tip

If you have a choice of plays, choose the one most likely to prevent your opponent from going out. For example, if you suspect he has the Ace of Hearts, and you have the 2, you will hold it back so that he is unable to play that card.

Snip, Snap, Snorem

The Object of the Game
To get rid of all your cards.

The Deal
Deal one card at a time to each player, until the pack is used up. It doesn't matter if some players have more cards than the others.

The Play
The player to the left of the dealer puts any card faceup on the table. The next player to the left matches it with the same card in a different suit, saying "Snip."

The next player to the left matches the original card with the same card in a third suit, saying "Snap." The next player follows with the fourth card of the same kind, saying "Snorem." If a player is unable to follow with a matching card, he says "Pass," and his turn goes to the next player to the left.

Let's say that Allan puts down a 6 of Hearts. The next player to the left, Bette, has no 6 and therefore must say "Pass." Carol, the next player, has the 6 of Diamonds and puts it down, saying "Snip." Dennis, the player to the left, has both of the remaining 6s and puts them down one at a time, saying "Snap" for one and "Snorem" for the other.

Then Dennis (the player who said "Snorem,") after putting down the fourth card of a kind, plays the first card of the next group of four. If he has more than one of a kind, he must put down as many as he has instead of holding out one of the cards for "Snorem."

For example, if you decide to put down Kings, and you have two of them, you must put both of them down at the start. You're allowed to put down just one of them and wait for the other two Kings to appear before showing your remaining King for a "Snorem."

The first player to get of his cards wins the game.

The Earl of Coventry

This is the same as "Snip, Snap, Snorem," except that different words are used. The exact word depends on how old the player is. Young children always use the same words when putting down their cards.

Suppose a young player puts down a 5. He says, "There's as good as 5 can be." The next player to put down a 5 can say, "There's a 5 as good as he." The next player says, "There's the best of all the three." The fourth player says triumphantly, "And there's the Earl of Coventry!"

Adult players need to make a different rhyming statement as they play their cards.

For example, an adult who plays a 6 might say, "Here's a 6 you can have from me," or "The best 6 now on land or sea," or any other rhyme.

If an adult fails to make an acceptable rhyming statement when he plays his card, he is not allowed to begin a new series. The turn passes to the player at his left.

Jig

This is the same game as "Snip, Snap, Snorem," except that the players put down four cards in sequence instead of four of a kind.

For example, suppose that the player to the left of the dealer begins by putting down a 5. The next player must put down any 6 or must pass. The next player must put down any 7 or pass. The play is completed by the next person who puts down any 8. The one who completes the play with the fourth card in sequence then begins the new series.

The game may be played by saying "Snip, Snap, Snorem," or with rhymes, as in "The Earl of Coventry."

# of players: 2–8

This game is best for two, three, or four players. In a four-handed game, the players who sit across the table from each other are partners.

The Object of the Game
To get rid of all your cards. The first player to get rid of them wins.

The Deal
Deal out seven cards to each player in a two-handed game, five to each player when more than two are playing.

Put the rest of the cards on the table facedown as the stock. Turn the top card faceup to begin another pile.

The Play
The player to the left of the dealer must match the card that has been turned up. That means he

must put down a card of the same suit or of the same rank.

For example, suppose that the card first turned up is the 9 of Spades. The first player needs to put down another Spade or a 9. That card is placed on top of the turned-up card. It is up to the next player to match the new card either in suit or in rank.

The four 8s are wild, which means that you may play an 8 at any time when it is your turn. When putting down an 8, you are allowed to call it any suit at all, as you please.

For example, you might put down the 8 of Hearts and say "Spade." The next player would then have to follow with a Spade.

If, at your turn, you cannot play, you must draw cards from the top of the stock until you are able to play or until there are no more cards left. You are allowed to draw cards from the stock at your turn, even if you are able to play without drawing. This is sometimes a good idea.

Sometimes a hand ends in a block, with nobody able to play, and with nobody having played out. The hand is then won by the player with the smallest number of cards. If two or more players tie for this honor, the hand is declared a tie.

Strategy

The most important principle is not to play an 8 too quickly. If you waste an 8 when you are not really in trouble, you won't have it to save you when the going gets tough.

The time that you really need an 8 to protect yourself is when you have been run out of a suit.

For example, after several Spades have been played, you might not be able to get another Spade, even if you drew every single card in the stock.

If you are also unable to match the rank of the card that has been put down, you may be forced to pick up the entire stock before your turn is over. From here on, of course, it will be very hard for you to avoid a disastrous defeat. An 8 will save you from this kind of misfortune, since you can put it down in place of a Spade, and you may be able to call a suit that does for your opponent what the Spade would have done for you.

If you're lucky, you won't have to play the 8 as your next to last card. It would be better to play it when your next turn comes—and win the hand. To play an 8 with more than two cards in your hand is seldom wise. It is usually a good idea to draw a few cards from stock in order to find a playable card.

Tip

The best way to beat an opponent is to run her out of some suit. If you have several cards in one suit, chances are your opponent will not have so many. As often as you get the chance, keep coming back to your long suit, until your opponent is unable to match your card. Eventually, she will have to draw from stock and may have to load herself up badly before she is able to play.

Hollywood Eights

# of players: 2–8

This is the same as "Crazy Eights," except that you keep score in points with pencil and paper.

When a hand comes to an end, each loser counts up his cards as follows:

Point Value of the Cards

Each 8 = 50
Each King, Queen, Jack, or 10 = 10
Each Ace = 1
Each other card = its face value

The winner of a hand gets credit for the total of all points lost by the other players.

For example, suppose you have an 8, a 9, and a 7 when a hand ends. The 8 counts 50 points, the 9 counts 9, and the 7 counts 7. The total is 50 + 9 + 7 or 66 points.

Hollywood Scoring

Three separate game scores are kept. The first time a player wins a hand, his score is credited to him in the first game column. The second time he wins a hand, he gets credit for his victory in both the first game column and the second. The third time a player wins, his score is credited to him in all three game columns. He continues to get credit in all three games from then on.

Sometimes a game runs on until everybody feels like stopping. Then, the three game scores are added up, and the winner is the player with the biggest total for the three scores. Suppose you win five hands in a row, with scores of 10, 25, 20, and 28 points. Your score would look like this:

FIRST GAME	SECOND GAME	THIRD GAME
10	25	40
(+25) 35	(+40) 65	(+20) 60
(+40) 75	(+20) 85	(+28) 88
(+20) 95	(+28) 113	
(+28) 123		

100 Scoring

A more popular way to end a game is to stop as soon as any player's score reaches 100.

When this happens in the first of the three games, the other two games continue. In later hands, the score is entered on the second game and third game, but no further entry is made in the finished first game. Sooner or later, some player reaches a score of 100 in the second game, and this likewise comes to an end. Eventually, also some player reaches a score of 100 in the third game, and then all three games have ended.

The winner is the player with the highest total score when all three game scores have been added up.

# of players: 2 or more

The Object of the Game
To get rid of all your cards.

The Deal
Deal seven cards to each player. Put the rest of the pack facedown in the middle of the table.

The Play
The player to the left of the dealer puts any card on the table. The next player to her left must follow by matching the suit or rank of that card. Each player in turn after this must match the previous card in suit or rank.

For example, suppose the first player puts down the Jack of Diamonds. The next player may follow with any Diamond or with another Jack. If the second player decides to follow with the Jack of Clubs, the third player may then match with a Club or with one of the two remaining Jacks.

When a player cannot match the previous card, he must draw cards from the stock until he is able to play. If a player uses up the stock without finding a playable card, he may say "Pass," and his turn passes to the next player.

When everybody at the table has had the chance to play or say "Pass," the cards are examined to see who has played the highest card.

The cards rank as follows:

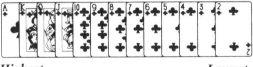

Highest   **Lowest**

The player who put down the highest card has the right to begin the next play. If there is a tie for first place among cards of the same rank, the card that was played first is considered higher.

The play continues until one player gets rid of all his cards and wins the hand.

If you want to use a system of point scoring, have each loser count the cards left in his hand as follows:

Each picture card	10
Each Ace	1
Each other card	its face value

The winner of the hand is credited with the total of all points lost by the other players.

Strategy

The strategy in "Go Boom" is much the same as in "Crazy Eights." You try to run your opponent out of a suit in hopes that he will not be able to match your play with a card of the same suit or the same rank.

In the early stages of play it is useful to put down as high a card as possible in order to have the best chance to win the privilege of beginning the next play.

Hollywood Go Boom

This is the same game as "Go Boom," except that the scoring is Hollywood style (three games at a time. As in "Hollywood Eights," three game scores are kept for each player. The first time you win a hand, you get credit only in your first game score. The second time you win a hand, you get credit both in your first and second game score. After that you get credit in all three.

The first game ends when any player reaches a score of 100. Later hands are scored only in the second and third games. The second game also ends when any player reaches a score of 100. After that, the scores are entered only in the third game score, and when some player reaches a score of 100 in that game, all the scores are totalled to see who wins.

# of players: 4–6

When four people play this game, use the Ace, King, Queen, Jack, 10, 9, 8, and 7 of each suit. If a fifth person plays, add 6s and 5s. If there is a sixth player, add the 4s and 3s. You need eight cards for each player.

The Object of the Game

To get rid of all your cards.

The Deal

Deal one card at a time until each player has eight cards. This uses up the pack.

The Play

The player to the dealer's left begins by putting down any card he pleases. Then the play moves to the left and the next player puts down another card in the same suit.

The turns continue, always moving to the left, with the other players following with another card of the same suit, if they can, playing high or low, as they please.

If all the cards in a suit are played, the person who put down the highest card leads again. And all the cards that were played to this first "trick" (sequence of cards) are turned over and put aside. For the purpose of winning a trick, the cards rank as follows:

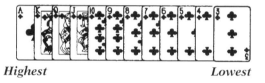

Highest   **Lowest**

When a player cannot put down a card of the same suit when it's her turn to play, she must pick up all the cards previously played in that sequence. This ends the trick. She then begins the next trick by leading with any card she chooses.

The process continues. In most games, a player picks up the cards several times. Eventually, one player will get rid of all his cards, and win the hand.

7
The
Casino Family

Casino

This game is best with two players.

The Object of the Game

To win the highest number of points. You get points by capturing the most cards, the most Spades, Aces, the 10 of Diamonds (Big Casino), and the 2 of Spades (Little Casino).

The Deal

The deck of 52 cards is used up in six deals. In the first deal:

- The non-dealer receives two cards face-down.
- Then two cards are put faceup on the table.
- Then the dealer gives himself two cards facedown.

And the process repeats, so that each player and the table have four cards each.

In the remaining five deals, the dealer continues to give each player four cards—two at a time—but does not give any additional cards to the table.

The Play

Beginning with the non-dealer, each player in turn must play one card from his hand, until all four of his cards are gone. If he can find no better use for it, he simply places his card faceup on the table. This is called *trailing*. Whenever he can, though, he uses his card to capture cards from the table.

Pairing

You may win cards in various ways. The simplest way is by pairing. You may capture a card on the table with another of the same rank from your hand—a 5 with a 5, a Jack with a Jack, and so on. With a picture card—a Jack, Queen, or King— you may capture only one card, but with a card of lower rank, you may take two or three of the same kind at the same time. If there are two 7s on the table and you have a 7 in your hand, for example, you can take all three.

Each player keeps captured cards in a pile, facedown.

Building

All the lower cards—Ace to 10—may be captured by building. Ace counts as 1. Each other card counts as its own value. Cards on the table may be taken in by higher cards to equal their sum.

For example, you may take a 5 and a 2 with a 7. You may take an Ace and a 9 with a 10. You may, at the same time, take additional cards by pairing. Suppose that the cards on the table are 9, 8, 5, 4, and Ace. You could take them all with a single 9, since the 9s pair up, 8 and 1 make 9, and 5 and 4 make 9.

Leaving a Build

Suppose that you have 8 and 3 in your hand, and

there is a 5 on the table. You may put the 3 on the 5 and say, "Building 8." Your intention is to capture the build with your 8 on your next turn, because you are allowed to play only one card from your hand at a time.

If your opponent has an 8, she can capture your build. That's the risk of leaving a build. Yet the risk is usually worth taking, because in building, you make it harder for your opponent to capture cards. She cannot take the 5 or the 3 by pairing or by making a build of her own.

Of course, you may not leave a build unless you have a card in your hand that can take it. You are, however, allowed to duplicate your build before taking it in. Suppose you have two 8s in your hand. After building the 5 and 3, you could on your next turn simply put one 8 on the build, and take it with the other 8 on your third turn.

Or suppose—after you build the 5 and 3, your opponent trails a 6, and you have a 2 in your hand (besides the 8), You may take your 2 and put it, along with the 6, on the 5-3 build, and wait until your next turn to take in the duplicated build.

An important rule is that when you have left a build on the table, you must deal with it at your next turn—take it in—or increase or duplicate it. You are not allowed to trail or to take in other cards instead.

Increasing a Build

Suppose that your opponent has laid a 4 from her hand on a 5 on the table, and called out, "Building 9." You have an Ace and a 10. You may add the Ace to her build and say "Building 10." You are allowed to increase a build of your own in the same way.

But there are two restrictions on increasing a build. First, you may increase only a *single* build, such as the 5-4—not one that has been duplicated in any way—such as 5-4-9. Second, the card you use to increase it must come from your hand, not from the table.

Scoring

After the last card of the sixth deal is played, any cards remaining on the table go to the player who was last to capture cards. Then each player looks through his captured cards and counts up his score, as follows:

Cards: for winning 27 or more cards	3 points
Spades: for winning 7 or more Spades	1 point
Big Casino: the 10 of Diamonds	2 points
Little Casino: the 2 of Spades	1 point
Aces: each counting 1	4 points
Total of	11 points

The first one to reach a total of 21 or more points wins.

Spade Casino

This is "Casino" with a different count for Spades. Instead of getting one point for having seven or more Spades, the Spades score as follows:

Jack:	2
Little Casino:	2
Other Spades:	1 each

In this game there are 24 points to be won. The game is usually set at 61 and scored on a Cribbage board.

Sweep Casino

In this version of "Casino," there is an additional rule. A player scores one point for each *sweep*. You earn this by capturing all the cards on the table at any one time. To keep track of sweeps, turn the top card of each sweep face up.

Winning the cards left on the table after the last deal does not count as a sweep.

Pirate Casino

The "pirate" feature is that you are allowed to make any play you please at a time when you have left a build on the table. You may take in other cards or even trail.

Stealing Bundles

This is "Casino" for the very young.

The Object of the Game
To win more than half the cards.

The Play
Cards may be captured only by pairing, but any number of the same kind may be taken at a time. Captured cards must be kept in a pile face up, and you can capture your opponent's entire pile by matching its top card with a card from your hand.

Children often prefer this colorful elaboration on the basic game of "Casino." Since this version is more complicated, young children should learn the basic game before attempting it.

In this game, you may capture picture cards as well as lower cards two, three, and four cards at a turn. Furthermore, they can be used to capture builds.

Point Value of the Cards

Jack counts:	11
Queen counts:	12
King counts:	13
Ace counts:	14 or 1, as you wish.
Little Casino:	15 or 2
Big Casino:	16 or 10

Sweeps are scored as in "Sweep Casino."

Partnership Casino

# of players: 4 (the two opposite being partners)

The Deal

The deck is used up in three deals. In the first, each one of the four players receives four cards and four are dealt faceup on the table. For the other two deals, each receives four more cards, but no more are dealt to the table.

Otherwise, this game is played just like "Casino" (basic or Royal) except that you may duplicate a build left by your partner without you yourself having a card that can take it.

For example, if Tom builds 10, Nellie, his partner, may in turn put a 6 from the table and a 4 from her hand on the build, without having a 10 in her hand.

You can play either basic "Casino" or "Royal Casino" in "Draw" style.

After you deal, place the rest of the pack face-down in the middle of the table. Each time you play a card, draw the top card of this stock, so that you keep four cards in your hand throughout the game. After the stock is exhausted, play out the hands as usual.

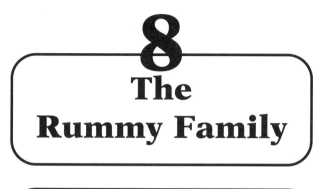

8
The
Rummy Family

Basic Rummy

# of players: 2–6

The Object of the Game

To win points from your opponents. To do this, you have to match up your cards by getting three or four of a kind, or sequences of cards that are next to each other in rank and the same in suit.

For example, you could match up three Kings or four 10s, or a sequence of cards like:

Highest ... *Lowest*

or

A typical sequence

Another typical sequence

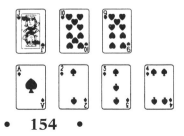

You need at least three cards for a sequence.

The Deal

Deal ten cards to each player when two are playing; seven cards to each when three or four are playing, and six cards to each person when five or six are playing.

Put the rest of the cards facedown in the middle of the table, forming the stock. Turn the top card faceup, starting the discard pile.

The Play

Each player at the table plays in turn, beginning with the player to the dealer's left. In your turn, you do three things:

You draw a card from the stock.
You meld, if you can.
You discard.

When you draw, you may pick up the top card of the stock or the top card of the discard pile. You add this card to your hand.

To meld, you put a group of matched cards

down on the table, if you are lucky enough to have three or four of a kind or of a sequence.

You don't have to put them down, though. You can keep them in your hand, if you want.

You can also, on your turn, add to any meld that is out on the table.

For example, if someone has put down three Kings, you may add the fourth King when it is your turn to play. If someone has put down the 6, 7, and 8 of Diamonds, you could add the 9 and 10 of Diamonds, or the 5 and 4, or any such card or group of cards.

After you have drawn and melded—or after you have declined to meld—it is your turn to discard. You can take any card from your hand and put it on top of the faceup pile in the middle of the table. This completes your turn.

If, on your turn, you manage to meld all your cards, you win the game. You must begin your play with a draw, thus adding one card to your hand, and then you must meld either all the cards in your hand, or all but one, which would be your discard.

If no player has melded all his cards (called "going out") by the time the stock is used up, the next player may take either the top card of the discard pile or the top card of the new stock that has been formed by turning the discard pile over. In either case, the game goes on as before, until somebody does go out.

Scoring

The winner of a hand scores points by counting up the hands of all the other players in the game. Each loser counts the cards in his hand according to the following scale:

Point Value of the Cards

Picture cards = 10 points each
Aces = 1 point each
Other cards = face value

A loser does not count cards that he has previously melded on the table, but he does count any cards that remain in his hand—*whether or not these cards match!*

When you meld all your cards in one turn, without previously melding or adding to anybody else's meld, it is called "going Rummy." Whenever you "go Rummy," you win double the normal amount from each of the other players.

Keep score with pencil and paper, setting up a column for each player. Whenever a player wins a hand, put the amounts that he wins from the other players into his winning column.

Some players agree on a stopping time when they play "Rummy." The winner is the player with the highest score when that time is up. Other players end a game when any player reaches a certain total score, such as 500 points. The score for each player is added up at the end of each hand.

Strategy

In all games of the Rummy family, you try to build up your hand by keeping cards that match and discarding cards that don't.

For example, if you drew the 10 of Spades, you would tend to keep it if your hand contained one or more 10s, or the Jack of Spades or the 9 of Spades. Even if it did not immediately give you a meld, it would probably bring you closer to one.

If you drew a card that didn't match anything in your hand, you would either discard it immediately, or wait for a later chance to discard it.

If the player to your left picks up a card from the discard pile, this gives you a clue to what's in his hand. If, for example, he picks up the 9 of Diamonds, you know that he must have other 9s or other Diamonds in the neighborhood of the 9. If convenient, you might avoid throwing another 9 or another Diamond in that vicinity onto the discard pile.

This is called "playing defensively." You don't need to bother with defensive play against anybody but the player to your left, since your discard would be covered up by the time any other player wanted to draw.

The advantage of melding is that you cannot

lose the value of those cards, even if some other player wins the hand.

The advantage of holding a meld in your hand is that nobody can add to the meld while it is still in your hand. A second advantage is the possibility of going "Rummy" all in one play.

It sometimes pays to hold up a meld, but most successful Rummy players make it a habit to put melds down fairly quickly. It's usually safe to hold up a meld for one to two turns, but after that it's dangerous. If another player goes out before you have melded, you will lose those matched cards just as though they were unmatched.

Block Rummy

This is the same as "Basic Rummy," except after you have gone through the stock once, the discard pile is not turned over to begin again. Instead, the next player has the right to take the top card of the discard pile. If she does not wish to take it, the hand ends immediately. This is called a "block."

When a block occurs, each player shows his hand. The player with the lowest number of cards in his hand wins the difference in value between his hand and the hands of the other players. If there is a tie for the lower number of points, the players share the winnings equally.

Boathouse Rummy

This is just like "Basic Rummy," except that sequences go "around the corner."

For example, you may meld

as a sequence.

But you are not allowed to meld anything at all until you can meld your whole hand and go out. When you go out, you win points from every other player according to his unmatched cards—that is, the cards in his hand that he has not matched up in groups of three of four or in sequences.

Scoring

There are two methods. One is to count one point

for each unmatched card. The other is to count:

11 for an unmatched Ace
10 for a face card
face value for all other cards

Special Feature

When you begin your turn, if you draw the top card of the discard pile, you may then draw a second card—from the discard pile or from the stock, whichever you please. If you begin by drawing from stock, however, you don't get a second card.

Knock Rummy

The game is the same as "Basic Rummy," except:

The Deal
When two people are playing, ten cards to each.
When three or four are playing, seven cards to each.
When five or six are playing, five cards to each.

The Play
There is no melding until somebody knocks. To "knock" means to lay down your whole hand faceup, ending the play. You may knock in your turn after drawing, but before discarding. You don't have to have a single meld in order to knock, but you'd better be sure that you have the low hand.

When anybody knocks, all players lay down their hands, arranged in the melds they have, with the unmatched cards separate. What counts is the total of the unmatched cards.

If the knocker has the lowest count, he wins the difference of counts from each other player.

If he lays down a "rum hand"—one with no unmatched cards—he wins an extra 25 points from everybody, besides the count of the unmatched cards from each other player.

If someone else beats or ties the knocker for low count, that player wins the difference from everybody else.

When the knocker is beaten, he pays an extra penalty of 10 points.

It's best to keep score with paper and pencil. Each item needs to be entered twice—*plus* for the winner and *minus* for the loser.

Tunk

# of players: 2–5

This is the same game as "Basic Rummy," except:

The Object of the Game
To go out. You don't need to meld all your cards, but merely to reduce the total value of your unmatched cards to five or less.

The Deal
Use one pack with two or three players. Use two packs with four or five players. Each player receives seven cards.

The Play
Before going out, you must give notice by saying "Tunk," in your turn—and that is all you can do in your turn.

A tunk takes the place of draw-meld-discard. Then the other players unload all that they can from their hands and on your next turn you lay down your hand, ending the play. You may at any time add cards to your own melds, or to a tunker's melds after the tunk, but not on the melds of another player.

The tunker scores zero, and the others are charged with the count of all cards left in their hands. When a player reaches 100, he is out of the game and the others play on until there is only one survivor.

Special Feature

2s are wild and may be used in place of other cards to form melds.

Gin Rummy

The Object of the Game

To reduce the count of your unmatched cards. A matched set in "Gin" is the same as a "meld" in "Basic Rummy": three or four cards of the same rank, or in sequence in the same suit: For example, here are two matched sets:

In "Gin," Aces rank low:

Highest   *Lowest*

This is a sequence.   **This is not.**

Point Value of the Cards:

Ace	1
Picture cards	10
Other cards	face value

The Deal

Each player gets ten cards, dealt one at a time. Place the rest of the deck facedown in the middle of the table to form the stock. Turn over the top card of the stock beside it. This upcard starts the discard pile.

The Play

The non-dealer plays first. If she wants the upcard she may take it, but if she doesn't, she must say so without drawing. Then the dealer may take it if he wants, and discard one card from his hand, face-up. After he has taken or refused it, the non-dealer continues with her turn, drawing one card—the top card of the stock or the card that the dealer has just discarded. Then she discards one card faceup on the discard pile and the play continues with no further complications.

Knocking

All melding is kept in the hand until some player brings matters to a halt by laying down all his ten cards, either by "ginning" or "knocking."

To gin, you lay down all your cards in melds. When you knock, you have unmatched cards whose total is ten or less. You may knock only when it is your turn to play, after drawing and before discarding. The final discard is made facedown, indicating the intention to knock. If you simply placed the card faceup, you could be stopped, because—according to the rules—the faceup discard would end your turn.

As you play, you arrange your cards in matched sets with the unmatched cards to one side. It is customary to announce the total count or your unmatched cards by saying something like, "Knocking with five." Your opponent then shows her hand. She is entitled to lay off cards on your sets, provided that you don't have a gin hand—all ten cards—matched.

For example, if you had this hand:

Knock Hand

your opponent could lay off the fourth Jack and the 10 and 6 of Hearts, if she had any of those cards.

Scoring

Your opponent counts her remaining unmatched cards after laying off what she can onto your hand. If the count is higher than yours, you win the difference. If your opponent has the same count that you have—or a lower one—she scores the difference, if any, plus 25 points for under-cutting you.

If you lay down a gin hand, your opponent may not lay off any cards on it. You win your opponent's count plus a bonus of 25 points. You can't win that bonus if you knock.

Keeping Score

Keep score with pencil and paper. Enter the result of hand in the column under the winner's name. Draw a line below the item and then write the running total. The lines between the items are important, to keep track of how many hands were won by each player. Each player is credited with 25 points for each winning hand. This is called the "line" or "box score."

If you are the first player to reach a total of 100 or more, you win the game and score a bonus of 100 points.

If your opponent has not scored a single point, that is a "shutout"— or a "whitewash," "skunk," "Schneider," "goose egg," etc., and you get an additional 100 points for that.

Oklahoma Gin Rummy

This is "Gin Rummy" except that the upcard determines the maximum number with which you can knock.

For example, if you turn up a 3 from the stock at the beginning, it takes 3 or less to knock in that deal. If you turn up a 10 or a picture card, the game is no different from regular "Gin."

Some players like to pep up the game with additional rules, such as: The hand counts double when the upcard is a Spade.

Gimme

The Object of the Game

To be first to get rid of all the cards in your hand.

The Deal

You need two decks of cards—with jokers—shuffled together. If you have seven or more players, use three decks of cards.

Deal eleven cards to each player. The dealer puts the rest of the pack in the center of the table and turns the top card faceup. Each game consists of seven hands; each one begins in the same way. The player to the dealer's left may take that card. If she doesn't want it, any player who does may say "Gimme." The one closest to the dealer gets it, but he must take the top facedown card along with it.

The Play

Each player in turn picks a card from the top of the deck and discards one into a separate discard pile faceup beside the deck. The player to his left may pick up the discard, but if he does not, other players may say "Gimme" and the game goes on as above.

You are allowed only three "Gimme's" in any hand (which means you may get a maximum of 17 cards). At your turn, you may meld cards according to the following rules:

First hand: Two sets
Second Hand: One set, one sequence
Third Hand: Two sequences
Fourth Hand: Three sets
Fifth Hand: Two sets, one sequence
Sixth Hand: Two runs, one sequence
Seventh Hand: Three runs

The sets and sequences for each hand do not have to be laid down at the same time.

Jokers are wild and may substitute for any card in a sequence or a set.

At your turn, you may also put down cards that add onto the melds already on the table.

For example, if there is a set of sevens on the table, you can meld a 7 from your own hand. If there is a run of Hearts from the 2 to the 5, you could meld an Ace of Hearts or a 6 from your hand.

A hand ends as soon as one player has no more cards. Other players total the value of all the cards left in their hands. These count against them.

Point Value of the Cards

Joker = 50 points
Ace = 25 points
Jack, Queen, King = 10 points each
All other cards = 5 points

The winner is the player with the lowest score after all seven hands have been played.

# of players: 2-4

Also known as "Open Rummy," this is one of the best rummy games. It is thoroughly involving and fast-moving. It keeps you on your toes, always engaged in planning strategies.

The Object of the Game

To lay out sets and sequences in order to be the first to get rid of all your cards.

The Deal

You need two decks of 52 cards (no Jokers) shuffled together. Deal seven cards to each player and put the deck in the middle of the table.

The Play

Each player, in turn, takes the top card off the deck and adds it to his hand. After picking a card, a player may meld.

Possible melds are three or more cards of the same value), or three same-suit cards in sequence (like 2, 3, 4 of Spades). If the person cannot meld, play passes to the left.

At any turn a player may put down all possible melds, add to sets or sequences on the table, and rearrange them. You can take them apart and put them down in a new way, as long as the result leaves you with a set or sequence of at least three cards.

For example, let's say there's a sequence of Jack-Queen-King-Ace of Diamonds on the table, and also a run of 8, 9, 10, and Jack of Spades. And you have a Jack of Hearts in your hand. You can remove the Jack of Diamonds and the Jack of Spades from the runs that they are in, and put them down with the Jack of Hearts to make a set of Jacks.

Rearrangements may involve many different sets and sequences. When all possible moves have been made, the player knocks on the table to indicate that the next player may take his turn. Play continues until one player has no more cards and is the winner of the hand.

The other players count up the value of the cards remaining in their hands. Those points are credited to the score of the player who won the hand. At the end of an agreed upon number of hands, the player with the highest score is the winner of the game.

Point Value of the Cards

All cards, Ace-10 = face value
Ace = 1 point
Face cards = 10 points each

However, Aces can be high or low, so runs could include these possibilities:

Ace, 2, 3
Queen, King, Ace
King, Ace, 2

Drat!

# of players: 2–4 or more

Here's another version of rummy. This one is from England.

The Object of the Game

To be first to get rid of all the cards in your hand.

The Deal

You'll need two decks of cards with jokers. Wild cards are jokers and twos. If there are five or more players, use three decks.

Deal eleven cards to each player. Put the remaining cards in the center of the table and turn up the top card.

Special Rules

A game consists of twelve or more hands. There are twelve "contracts" to be made in turn. Each player must make contract #1 before he can make #2, even if other players are on a second or third.

Here are the twelve contracts:

#1 Two sets of three (cards of the same value)

#2 One set of three, one sequence of four (a
run of cards of the same suit in sequence)

#3 Two sets of four

#4 Two sequences of four

#5 One set of four, one sequence of four

#6 Three sets of three

#7 One set of three, sequence of four

#8 Two sets of three, one sequence of four

#9 Two sets of five

#10 One sequence of five

#11 One sequence of eight

#12 One sequence of ten.

In any set or sequence, you can't have more
wild cards than regular cards.

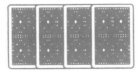

Aces may be high (following a King in a sequence) or low (before a two).

The Play

The player to the dealer's left may pick up the turned-up card, or take the top card of the face-down pack.

When he has taken a card, he discards one on the faceup pile. The next player may take either the top faceup card or the top facedown card—and then discards one. Play proceeds to the left. At your turn, you may meld cards in keeping with your contract. You don't have to meld the entire contract at once.

For example, if you have to make two sets, you can lay down one at a time.

After a contract is made, the other cards in the hand can be placed on contracts already on the table.

For example, a 2 can be placed on a set of 2s, or a 10 of Spades on a run of 6, 7, 8, 9 of Spades.

When a player gets rid of all his cards, other players' remaining cards count against them.

Point Value of the Cards

Joker = 50 points

2 = 50 points

Ace = 25 points

9 to King = 10 points

3-8 = 5 points

Scoring

When the first player goes out after the 12th contract has been made, the winner is the player with the lowest score—even if that player has not completed Contract #12.

Frustration

This version of rummy is played just like "Drat!," except twelve cards are dealt to each player. The only wild cards are jokers and the scoring is different. In addition, you have to make ten contracts:

#1 Two sequences of three

#2 One set of three, one sequence of three

#3 One sequence of four, one set of four

#4 Two sequences of four

#5 One sequence of four, two sets of three

#6 One sequence of five, one set of three

#7 One sequence of seven, one set of three

#8 Two sequences of four, one set of three

#9 Four sets of three

#10 Two sequences of five

Penalty Points

Here are the penalty points for cards left in the hand when the game is over:

Joker = 20 points
Ace = 15 points
10, Jack, Queen, King = 10 points each
2–9 = 5 points each

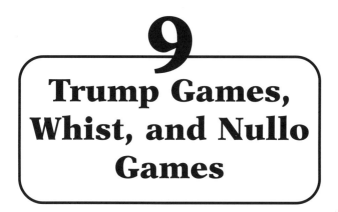

9
Trump Games, Whist, and Nullo Games

A trump suit is one that is given a special privilege. It can win over all the other suits. If Spades are trumps, for example, a 2 of Spades can win over the Ace of Hearts, even though the Ace of Hearts can win over any lower card.

In some games, the trump suit is picked by turning up a card from the deck. In other games the right to name the trump may be decided in another way.

About Nullo Games

In nullo games you need to *avoid* winning tricks, or to *avoid* taking certain cards. Most of them are easy to learn because they have practically no other rules.

# of players: 4–6

The Object of the Game

To get all the cards and be the last player left when everyone else has dropped out. If two or more players are down to one card each at the end, the winner of the last trick wins the game. (A trick is a round in which each person plays a card according to certain rules; these are different, depending on the game.)

The Deal

Each player receives as many cards as there are players in the game. for example, with five players, each receives five cards.

The last card dealt, which goes to the dealer, is shown to all the players. It decides the trump suit for that trick. The rest of the deck is placed face-down in the middle of the table, forming the stock.

The Play

The player to the left of the dealer makes the first "lead" (play), putting down in the middle of the table any card in the trump suit, if he can. Otherwise, he can put down any card he pleases. The other players "follow suit," putting down any cards in their hand that are in the trump suit. Each player tries to capture the trick of four cards by playing the highest card of the suit that was led.

When a player wins a trick, he "owns" those cards. Then he draws the top card of the stock, which determines the trump suit for the next trick.

When a player is left without any cards, he has to drop out of the game, and the others play on.

**# of players: 5–8
(6 is best)**

You need a handful of counters—toothpicks, pebbles, dried beans, etc. Give the same number to each player.

The Object of the Game

To win the most counters.

The Deal

Each player receives three cards, one at a time. An extra hand of three cards is dealt just to the left of the dealer. This is the "widow." If the player to the left of the widow does not like her hand, she may throw it away and take the widow instead. If she is satisfied with her hand, though, she must say so and stick with it.

Each player, in turn, has a chance to take the widow, until somebody takes it or all refuse it.

The Play (Single Pool)

After the matter of the widow is settled, the player to the left of the dealer makes the opening lead. You must always follow suit to the lead when you can. You must play a higher card than any other card in the trick, if you can. The highest card in the suit wins the trick. Aces are high.

Keep the tricks you have won faceup on the table in front of you as you play.

Trumps

The play begins without any trump suit and continues that way as long as everybody follows suit to every lead. When somebody fails to follow suit, the top card of the undealt stock is turned over. This card decides the trump suit. The trick that was just played is examined, and if a card that has been played turns out to be from the trump suit, that card wins the trick.

Scoring

To start a pool, the dealer must "ante up" three counters (put three of his counters in the middle of the table). When the pool contains no more than these three counters, it is a "single" and play takes place as before.

After the play, the pool pays out one counter for each trick won. Players who have not won a trick must pay three counters into the next pool, making it a "double pool"—or jackpot.

Double Pool

This is formed by the dealer's ante of three counters plus any payments for "loo"— not winning a trick in the previous hand.

After the deal, the next card of the deck is turned up, deciding the trump suit. After checking out their hands, the players must say in turn whether they will play or drop out. If all but the dealer drop out, he takes the pool. If only one player ahead of the dealer decides to play, the dealer must play too. He may play for himself, in which case he may not take the widow, or he may play "to defend the pool," in which case he must throw away his hand and take the widow. When the dealer plays just to defend the pool, he neither collects nor pays any counters. The pool alone settles with his opponent.

The nearest active player to the left of the dealer leads first. The other rules of play are the same as in a single pool.

The double pool pays out one-third of its contents for each trick won. A player who stays in and does not win a trick, must pay three counters to the next pool.

# of players: 3–5

You play this game with only 32 cards. Remove all cards from 2 through 6 from the deck. They rank like this:

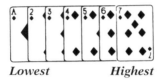

Lowest   **Highest**

You also need a handful of counters for this game, toothpicks, pebbles, dried beans, etc. Give the same number of counters to each player.

The Deal

Each player receives five cards in batches of three and two. An extra hand or "widow" is dealt, as in "Loo." The last card belonging to the dealer is turned up to decide the trump suit.

Declaring

After looking at their hands, the players in turn must declare whether they will play or drop out. If they play, they must undertake to win at least one trick. Any player in turn may discard his hand and take the widow instead, if it has not yet been taken.

Any player may declare rams: that he will undertake to win *all* the tricks. He may say this either before or after taking the widow, but must say it before the next player declares.

In a *rams* game, everybody must play: players who have dropped out must pick up their hands again.

If the rams player has not taken the widow, each player who has not refused it gets a chance to take it.

The Play

The player who declares rams makes the opening lead. Otherwise, it is made by the first player to the left of the dealer.

You must follow suit when you can, and you must play higher than any previous card in the trick, when you can. If a plain suit is led, you have to trump if you are able to, even if the trick has already been trumped. You must trump higher if you can. A trick is won by the highest trump in it, or if not trump, by the highest card of the suit led.

Scoring

The dealer antes up five counters. The pool may contain counters left from the previous deal.

Each player who has stayed in the game takes one counter (or one-fifth of all the counters) from the pool for each trick he wins. Players, as in "Loo," who win no tricks, must pay five counters into the next pool.

In a rams game, however, the settlement is different. If a rams player wins all the tricks, she wins the whole pool plus five counters from every player. If she loses a trick, the cards are thrown in at once. She must pay enough counters to double the pool and five counters to every player.

If everybody else passes, the player to the right of the dealer must pay him five counters if he wishes to drop. In this case, the pool remains undivided. If only one player other than the dealer decides to play, the dealer must play to defend the pool. In this case, he takes the trump card and discards another facedown.

# of players: 4 in partnerships

Whist is just about the simplest card game of all to play. What is not so simple is to play "Whist" well. The rules are simple and few. You can learn them in two minutes.

The Object of the Game
To win as many tricks as possible. Points for tricks and "honors" are accumulated, and the first side to reach a total of seven game points wins.

The Deal
Each player receives 13 cards, dealt one at a time. The last card of the pack, belonging to the dealer, is exposed to all the players. This card decides the trump suit for that hand.

The Rank
In every suit, the cards rank:

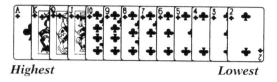

Highest   **Lowest**

The Play

The player to the left of the dealer makes the first lead. The hands are played out in tricks. You must follow suit to the lead, if you can. Otherwise, you may play or lead as you please. However, if a player *revokes*—by not following suit when he has in his hand an appropriate card to play—he and his partner have to pay a penalty. The penalty is decided upon before play begins, and may be as severe as two game points for the opponent. The partnership cannot win any trick in which it revokes.

A trick is won by the highest trump in it, or if it contains no trump, the highest card of the suit led. The winner of a trick makes the lead for the next trick.

One member of each partnership gathers together all the tricks won by his side. He doesn't throw them together in a single pile, but overlaps them crosswise, so that each batch of four cards remains separate from the others.

Scoring

The side that wins the majority of the tricks scores:

> 1 game point for each trick over six, and, if agreed upon, 2 game points should the opponents revoke.

In addition, points are scored for honors. The honors are the Ace, King, Queen, and Jack of the trump suit.

If 2 honors were dealt to each side, there is no score. If one side received 3 honors, it scores 2. For all 4 honors, the score is 4.

Remember that honors are scored by the side to which they are *dealt*, not won in play. Both sides may score in the same deal, one side winning a majority of tricks and the other side holding a majority of honors.

Dummy Whist

# of players: 3

The Deal

Played the same as "Whist," this game is not played in partnership. Four hands are dealt, as usual, with the extra hand—or dummy—going opposite the dealer.

The Play

The same as "Whist," except that the dealer plays the dummy hand as well as his own against the two live opponents.

Scoring

The dealer has a great advantage over his opponents, since he gets to see all 26 cards on his side. The fairest scoring method is to play three, six, or nine deals, so that each player has the same number of turns to deal. Then the player with the highest score is declared the winner.

# of players: 3

The Object of the Game

To make the number of tricks called for in each hand, and to be the first to score. (Players start with a score of 9. They gain or lose points depending on how many tricks they make.)

The Deal

Each player picks a card to decide the number of tricks he must make. The holder of the highest card must make nine tricks, the middle card five tricks, and the lowest card two tricks. If two players pick cards of the same value, they pick again. The holder of the highest card is the dealer. Aces are always high.

Deal out the entire deck to the three players, except for the last four cards. Place them facedown at the side. The dealer, after inspecting his cards, may choose to discard four and take the four facedown cards.

The Play

The player to the dealer's left plays any card. Other players must follow suit. The person with the highest card takes in the trick and leads to the next trick. If a player cannot follow suit, he can play any card. The game continues until all the cards have been played.

Scoring

Players count their tricks. The players each begin with a score of 9. If they make the number of tricks they are supposed to make (9, 5, or 2), their score goes down 2 points. For every trick over that number, they gain a point. For every trick under that number, they gain a point.

On the next deal (and all deals that follow), the number of tricks for each player changes: 9 becomes 2; 5 becomes 9; 2 becomes 5.

The game continues until one player reaches 0 and is the winner.

Four Jacks

# of players: 4, 5, or 6

You need a handful of counters for this game, toothpicks, pebbles, dried beans, etc. Give the same number to each player.

The Object of the Game

To avoid winning any Jacks. But before the opening lead, any player may announce that he will try to win all the tricks. This is called *capot*.

The Deal

With 4 players, use 32 cards—Ace to 7—discarding all 2s through 6s. Each player gets 8 cards.

With 5 or 6 players, use 30 cards —same as above, but discard the two black 7s. Each player receives 6 or 5 cards.

The Play

The player to the left of the dealer leads first. The hands are played out in tricks. There is no trump suit. Each trick is won by the highest card played of the suit led.

Scoring

Payments for holding Jacks and winning capot are made into a common pool, which is divided equally among all the players when the game ends. Whenever one player is down to his last counter, all players take equal numbers of counters from the pool.

If a capot is announced and made, every other player must pay five counters. But if the capot player fails to win all the tricks, he alone pays five counters.

When capot is not announced, the player who takes the Jack of Spades—called *Polignac*—must pay two counters into the pool. One counter must be paid for each of the other three Jacks taken in.

Slobberhannes

This game is played in much the same way as "Four Jacks," except here you want to avoid winning:

> the first trick
> the last trick
> the Queen of Clubs

Each of these costs one counter, and if you are unlucky enough to take all three, you must pay an extra counter—four in all.

# of players: 4

From Portugal, this is actually six different games played in sequence. Each is a good game in its own right. When you play it as a mega-game, the rules change with each new hand. You need to change your mindset continually and remember the objectives of the current hand.

The Object of the Game

To win or avoid tricks and key cards, depending on which hand is being played. The game consists of 12 hands. In the first six you get credit for key cards. In the next six, you lose credit for key cards.

The Deal

Players draw cards to decide who is the dealer. The first one to draw a King becomes the dealer of the first hand. After that, the deal passes to the person on the right.

All the cards are dealt out. The dealer, after looking at his cards, names the trump (the suit that will rank highest for this hand) or decides that there will be no trump.

The Play

The person to the dealer's right plays the first card. All players must put down a card of the same suit, if they can. The highest card takes all the others. If a player cannot play a card of the same suit, she can play a trump card, which wins over any other card. In the case of two trump cards, the higher trump wins the trick.

Rules for Individual Hands

POSITIVES The object of the game is to take in cards or tricks.

Hand 1: Score 25 for each trick taken.
Hand 2: Each Heart scores 20 points.
Hand 3: Score 50 points for each Queen
Hand 4: Score 30 points for each King and Jack.

Hand 5: Score 150 points for the King of Hearts.

Hand 6: Score 100 points for the next-to last trick, and 150 points for the last one.

• • • •

NEGATIVES: The object of the game is to avoid cards or tricks.

Hand 7: Lose 25 points for each trick.

Hand 8: Lose 20 points for each Heart.

Hand 9: Lose 50 points for each Queen.

Hand 10: Lose 30 points for each King or Jack.

Hand 11: Lose 150 points for the King of Hearts.

Hand 12: Lose 100 points for the next-to-last trick and 150 points for the last one.

The winner is the player with the highest score at the end of 12 hands.

10
The Hearts Family

Hearts

This is the basic and most simple of the Hearts family, though not the most popular. It is almost always played with four people; if you have more players, other forms of the game are better.

You also need a handful of counters for this game, toothpicks, pebbles, dried beans, etc., the same number to each player—or paper and pencil.

The Object of the Game
To avoid winning any hearts—or to win all 13 of them.

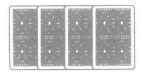

The Deal

Each player receives 13 cards. When you can't divide them equally, remove enough 2s from the deck to make deal come out even. Aces rank highest.

The Play

The player to the left of the dealer makes an opening lead and the cards are played in tricks. A trick is won by the highest card played of the suit led. There is no trump suit, though Hearts are often mistakenly called trumps. The winner of a trick leads to the next trick.

Scoring with counters

For each Heart that a player wins, he must pay one counter into the pool.

If two or more players take no Hearts, they divide the pool. But if all the players take Hearts, nobody wins the pool. It stays on the table as a jackpot and becomes part of the pool for the next deal.

Scoring with paper and pencil

Each Heart taken counts one point against the player. A game can be ended at any agreed-upon time, and the player with the lowest total score is the winner. If a player wins all the Hearts, the usual method of scoring is to deduct 13 from his score. Some people deduct double that—26, instead.

# of players: 3 or 5

The Deal

Place a widow (a group of cards) on the table—
four cards if three are playing, two cards if five
are playing. Deal out the rest of the cards.

The Play

Play in the same way as "Hearts," but turn the
widow face up after the first trick and it goes to
the winner of that trick. He must of course pay
for any Hearts it contains.

Spot Hearts

This variation on features a different scoring method that you can apply to any member of the Hearts family. The charges for taking Hearts go according to rank:

Point Value of the Cards

Ace counts	14
King counts	13
Queen counts	12
Jack counts	11
Others count	face value

This is "Hearts" with a Joker added.

The Deal

Add a Joker to the pack, discarding the 2 of Clubs to keep the deck at 52 cards.

Special Feature

The Joker can be beaten only by the Ace, King, Queen, or Jack of Hearts. Otherwise, it wins any trick in which it is played.

If you're playing "Heartsette," deal an extra card to the widow.

Scoring

The Joker counts as one Heart in payment, or in "Spot Hearts" scoring, it counts 20.

Domino Hearts

The Object of the Game

To have the lowest total when another player reaches 31 points.

The Deal

Each player gets 6 cards. The rest of the pack is put facedown in the middle of the table, forming the stock.

The Play

All tricks must be composed of cards of the same suit. There is no discarding. When a player is unable to follow suit to the lead, he must draw from the stock until he gets a playable card. After the stock is exhausted, he must pass.

When a player's hand is exhausted, he drops out of the deal and the others play on. If he should win a trick with his last card, the player to his left leads for the next trick.

When all but one have dropped out, the last player must add his remaining cards to his own tricks.

Hearts taken are charged at one point each.

Black Maria

Also called "Black Lady," this is the best known game of the Hearts family. It is what most people mean when they speak of "Hearts." It is best for four players, without partnerships.

You also need a handful of counters for this game, toothpicks, pebbles, dried beans, etc., the same number to each player, or pencil and paper for scoring.

The Object of the Game

To avoid taking the Queen of Spades, called Black Lady, Black Maria, Calamity Jane, etc., and to avoid taking Hearts, or else to take *all* the Hearts *and* the Queen of Spades—called "shooting the moon."

The Deal

Deal out the whole pack, giving equal hands to all.

With four players it works out right. With three players, discard a 2.

With five players, discard two 2s. With six players, discard four 2s. With seven players, discard three 2s.

The Pass

After looking at his hand, each player passes any three cards to the player to his left. He must choose which cards he is gong to pass and put them on the table before picking up the three cards passed to him by the player to his right.

The Play

The player to the left of the dealer makes the opening lead. The cards are played out in tricks. Aces rank highest. A trick is won by the highest card played of the suit led. The winner of a trick leads to the next trick.

Scoring

If one player takes all 14 "minus" cards—the 13 Hearts and the Queen of Spades—he can subtract

26 points from his score. Some people add 26 points to everyone else's score. Otherwise, one point is charged for each Heart won, and 13 points for the Queen of Spades.

A running total score is kept on paper for each player. The first one to reach 100 or more loses the game, and the one with the lowest total at that time wins.

When playing with young children, you may want a shorter game. In this case, set the limit at 50.

11
Solitaire
Games with One
Deck of Cards

Betsy Ross

The Layout

Lay out in the top row any Ace, 2, 3, and 4. Right under that, lay out any 2, 4, 6, and 8. The four cards on the bottom are foundations. You'll be building on them, but in an odd sort of way.

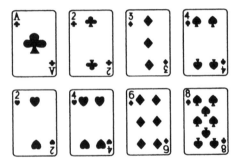

The Object of the Game

To build all the cards into groups of 13 on the foundations.

The only purpose of the top row is to remind you of the key numbers you have to build by.

The Play

On the 2 card, you'll build the regular way, by ones:

2 3 4 5 6 7 8 9 10 J Q K

On the 4 card, you'll build by twos:

4 6 8 10 Q A 3 5 7 9 J K

On the 6 card, you'll build by threes:

6 9 Q 2 5 8 J A 4 7 10 K

On the 8 card, you'll build by fours:

8 Q 3 7 J 2 6 10 A 5 9 K

Turn over the cards one by one, regardless of suit, building on any foundation that is ready for it. You get two re-deals, but that's all. If you've managed to build the whole deck onto the foundations, you've won.

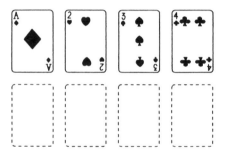

Calculation

This game is a lot like Betsy Ross.

The Layout
Remove any Ace, 2, 3, and 4 from the pack and set them up in a row. They are your foundations.

The Object of the Game
To build up all the foundations to Kings, each in a different way.

The Play

On the Ace, you'll build the regular way, by ones:

   A 2 3 4 5 6 7 8 9 10 J Q K

On the 2 card, you'll build by twos:

   2 4 6 8 10 Q A 3 5 7 9 J K

On the 3 card, you'll build by threes:

   3 6 9 Q 2 5 8 J A 4 7 10 K

On the 4 card, you'll build by fours:

   4 8 Q 3 7 J 2 6 10 A 5 9 K

Start by turning over one card at a time, which you can build, regardless of suit, on any foundation that is ready for it. If the card cannot be used on any pile, put it in one of four possible wastepiles underneath the foundations. The top cards of these wastepiles are available for play. The strategy you use to decide where to place the unusable card is crucial. It's okay to keep the cards spread out so you can see what your choices are at any moment. If you can build all the cards onto the foundations, you've won the game.

Canfield

"Canfield" is one of the most popular solitaire games in the world. A shorter, faster game than the equally popular "Klondike" (page 253), "Canfield" is played much the same way, but it starts from a different basic layout.

"Canfield" got its name in an interesting way. Mr. Canfield owned a gambling house in Saratoga Springs in the 1890s. He used to sell his customers packs of cards at $50 each, and then pay them back $5 for every card they were able to score. The average number of cards you could expect to score in a game was five or six, so Mr. Canfield did pretty well.

The Layout

Count out 13 cards into one pile and put it in front of you faceup and a little to your left. Then put a 14th card to the right of the pile, and slightly above it. Whatever that card is, it becomes the foundation card of this particular game. As the other cards of the same rank appear, you'll be placing them too in the foundation row.

Next you lay out a row of four cards below the foundation card, faceup.

The Object of the Game
To build the foundation cards into four complete suits of 13 cards each.

The Play
No cards are ever built on the 13-pile. The object is to unload it.

For example, in the illustration above, you couldn't put a 5—or any other card—on the 6.

Cards from the 13 pile can be played only onto the foundations or into the four card row when a space opens up.

First check the four-card spread carefully to see whether you can make any moves. Besides playing cards to the foundations, you can build cards onto the four-card row, one by one moving downwards, in alternating colors—first red, then black, then red, and so on.

For instance, in the diagram on page 231, the 3 of Hearts can go onto the 4 of Spades, the 7 of Diamonds can go up into the foundation row, and the 6 of Spades can come down from the 13-pile into the row of four. Once it does, you can play the 5 of Hearts onto it.

You are permitted to move sequences of cards as one unit.

For example, the 3 and 4 may be moved together onto the 5 and 6, so your layout would look like the one on page 233.

Then you can fill the other open spaces in the four-card row with cards from the 13-pile.

Now start turning up cards from the pack in batches of three, playing them either to the foundations, to the four-card row, or to the wastepile. You can always play the top card of the wastepile.

When the cards from the 13 card pile are gone, you can fill spaces in the four-card row with cards from your hand or from the wastepile. Redeal as many times as you want.

Selective Canfield

Play the same way as "Canfield," except deal a five-card row instead of four. Choose your foundation yourself from one of these cards.

Rainbow

Play the same way as "Canfield," except go through the pack one card at a time. You are allowed two re-deals in some versions of the game—none in others.

Storehouse

Play the same way as "Canfield," except:

1. Remove the four deuces from the pack and set them up as the foundations.
2. Build them up suit by suit to Aces.

Superior Demon

Play the same way as "Canfield," except:

1. Spread the 13-card pile so that you can see it and take it into account as you play.
2. You don't have to fill a space in the layout until you want.
3. You can shift any part of a sequence to another position—you don't have to move the entire sequence.

Chameleon

Play the same way as "Canfield," except:

1. Count out only 12 cards instead of 13 for the 13-card pile.
2. Deal a three-card row instead of the four-card row.
3. The layout looks slightly different, like this:

The Layout

Deal the pack into 13 piles of four cards each. Arrange 12 of them facedown in a circle, like the numbers on a clock face:

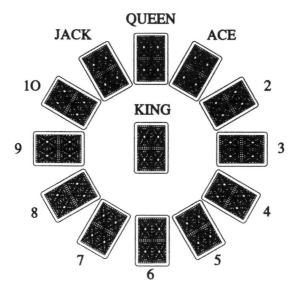

Put the 13th pile in the middle of the circle.

The Object of the Game

Get all the cards turned face up before the fourth King turns up.

The Play

Start by picking up the top card of the middle pile. Suppose it's a 5. Slip it, faceup, under the pile of cards that are in the 5 o'clock position. Then pick up the top card of the 5 o'clock pile.

Suppose it's a Jack. It would go under the 11 o'clock pile (remember, the King pile is in the middle of the clock and the Queen is at 12). And you would pick up the top card of the 11 o'clock pile and slip it under whatever pile it belongs in.

When you slip the fourth card of any group into place—and there is no facedown card to turn over—turn over the top card of the next highest card pile.

This is one of the most delightful solitaire games, but you need a lot of space for it..

The Layout

Lay out the whole deck in sets of three, faceup, like this:

One single card will be left over, which becomes a set of its own.

The only cards that may be moved are the exposed ones on top of the sets. They are built up on the foundation or on the top cards of other sets by suit, building downwards.

The Object of the Game

To release the Aces and build them up in suit to Kings.

The Play

Once you have the cards laid out, move the Aces that are available onto the foundations.

For example, in the layout on page 240, the Ace of Hearts can go on one of the foundations, so can the 2 and 3 of Hearts. Then the 3 of Spades can go onto the 4 of Spades, and so on.

Continue to build on the top cards of the three-leaf clovers, one card at a time. When a clover is entirely eliminated, it is not replaced.

Re-deals
You get two. To re-deal, gather up the clovers that are left, shuffle the cards, and set them down in groups of three as before. Any leftover cards are sets by themselves.

Special Bonus
In the last re-deal, when you're stuck, you get one free move—one card you can pull from underneath one or two others, and play in any way you want.

Super Flower Garden

Play the same way as "Clover Leaf," except building takes place regardless of suit.

Trefoil

Play the same way as "Clover Leaf," except you put the Aces in a foundation row before you start laying out the clovers. You'll then have 16 complete three-leaf clovers.

Shamrocks

Play the same way as "Clover Leaf" except:

1. If a King is on the top of a set and a card of lower rank in the same suit lies under it, you can put the King under that card.
2. No clover may contain more than three cards.

The Layout:

Lay out four fans of three cards each at the top of the table. Leave a space for the foundations, and then deal out a row of four cards. It will look like this:

The Object of the Game

Build the four foundation cards into full 13-card suits.

The Play

Choose any one of the exposed cards in the fans to be your foundation. For example, in the illustration on page 243, it might make sense to choose the 3 of Diamonds as your foundation, because the 3 of Spades is available to build onto the foundation, and so is the 4 of Diamonds.

After you make all possible moves to the foundations, you start moving downwards on the row of cards in alternating colors. You are allowed to move all the cards of one pile onto another pile as a unit, when the cards are in the right sequence (down by suit).

Go through the stockpile of cards one by one, building to the foundations or the layout—or discarding the unplayable cards to the wastepile.

When spaces open up in the row, fill them from the fans, and when no fans are left, from the wastepile.

The Layout

Deal 13 cards facedown in a pile in the middle of the table. This pile is known as "the trunk."

Then lay out four cards faceup on one side of the pile, and four cards faceup on the other. These are the "wings" of the eagle. Deal out one more card and place it directly above the pile, so your layout looks like this:

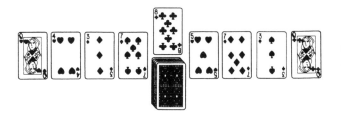

That last card is a foundation pile. As other 8s appear, they go up in a row alongside it, and you build on them as well.

Object of the Game

Build up the foundations to full 13-card suits.

The Play

Go through the cards one by one. If you can't play a card onto one of the foundation piles, put it in a wastepile. The top of the wastepile is always available for play.

You can also build with the cards in the wings. When a space opens up in the wings, fill it right away with a card from the trunk. The bottom card in the trunk—if you get that far—may be played directly to the foundation without waiting for a place in the wings.

In the building, Aces follow Kings.

You are allowed two re-deals (three times through the cards).

# of players: 2

This double solitaire game, a version of "Spit," is played by two people. As you can tell from its name, it is a very fast game!

The Object of the Game

To be the first to get rid of all your cards.

The Deal

Deal two facedown piles of four cards each, one to the right of each player. These are the starter cards. Deal out the rest of the deck so that each player has a facedown pile. Players take the top four cards of their facedown piles as their "hand," replacing cards as they are played, so that each player always has a four-card hand.

The Play

Both players turn up the top card of the starter

cards (to their right), placing the card faceup in the middle of the table, so that there are two cards side by side. These are the cards to be played upon.

Now, as fast as they can (no taking turns), the players try to play cards from their hands onto the faceup cards. A card may be played, regardless of suit, if it is one more or one less than the card on the table. So on a 7, you could play a 6 or an 8. On a King, you could play a Queen or an Ace. As plays are made, players take cards from their facedown pile, always keeping four cards in their hands.

When no more plays can be made, players again—at the same time—go to their starter cards, turn over the next card, put it into the middle of the table, and play resumes.

When the starter cards are used up, turn over the faceup playing cards in the middle of the table and use them to provide new starter cards.

Play continues until one player gets rid of all his cards and is the winner.

Grandma's Solitaire

The Layout

Deal four faceup cards in a square.

The Object of the Game

To remove all the cards and be left with only the four Aces.

Value of Cards

Aces are high.

The Play

If two or more faceup cards are of the same suit, remove the lower card. For example:

Remove the 5 of Hearts.

Deal four more cards, covering the cards in the layout or the spaces that remain. After each deal whenever there are cards of the same suit, remove the one that is lower in value. If a space becomes available, you can fill it with the top card of any pile. Deal out all the cards. The game is won when only the four Aces remain.

The Layout

Deal four cards faceup in a row.

The Object of the Game

To discard all the cards—except for the Aces.

The Play

If you have two cards that are of the same suit, discard the one that is lower in rank. Aces are high.

For example, here you have:

Discard the 5 of Hearts

When you've made all the moves you can, fill the empty space in the row with any top card from the layout. In this case, as there is only one layer of cards so far, fill the space from the cards in your hand. Then deal four more cards overlapping the ones you've already set up.

Keep going, discarding the lower card of the same suit from the new layer of cards, until you've gone through the whole pack. When you've discarded all the cards, except for the Aces, you've won the game.

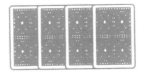

This is probably the most popular solitaire game in the world.

The Layout

Lay out seven cards in a row facedown except for the first card. Then put the eighth card face up on the second card in the row, and complete the row with facedown cards. Place a faceup card on the third pile, and finish off the row in the same way. Continue until you have a faceup card on every pile. Your layout will look like the diagram on the next page.

The Object of the Game

Build up complete suits from Ace to King.

The Play

First, look over the spread carefully. Move any cards that you can to the foundation row—Aces and any cards you can build on them.

You can also build cards on the layout. Only faceup cards are available for building, and only if they are the exposed cards of the pile. Then you can build downwards on them in alternating colors.

In the example shown here you can move the Ace up to the foundation row, and then move the black 3 onto the red 4, and the red 2 onto the black 3.

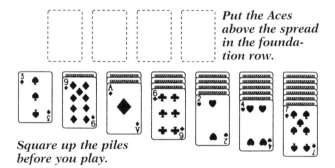

Put the Aces above the spread in the foundation row.

Square up the piles before you play.

Every time you move a faceup card, you turn up the facedown card beneath it. When there are no more facedown cards in a pile, you have a space. Spaces can be filled by any available King.

When you've made all the moves you can, start

going through the stockpile one by one, looking for more cards to build onto the foundations and the layout. If you can't place a card, it goes onto a wastepile, and the top card of the wastepile is available for play.

Scoring

Five rounds make a game. Add up the number of foundation cards you come up with in each round for your final score.

Klondike by Threes

This game is played the same as "Klondike," except you go through the stockpile of cards three at a time. Because of that, you get re-deals. Rules vary about how many re-deals you get. Some say two (three trips through the cards), and some say as many as you want.

Agnes

This game is played the same as "Klondike" except:

1. When you finish the layout, deal the next card above it to make the first foundation. Build the foundations in the same way you always do, but starting from that card. Aces get played between Kings and 2s.

2. Below the layout, deal a row of seven cards These are available to be played onto the layout and the foundations. Play as many of them as you can, and when you have no more moves to make, deal another seven cards on top of them. You'll probably have spaces in the row of seven. Be sure not to skip them when you deal the second row. After you deal a third layer of seven cards, you'll have two cards left in your hand. Turn them face up. They are available too.

3. Spaces in the layout may be filled by any card that is one lower than the foundation card. For example, if the foundation card is a 2, spaces can be filled only with Aces.

Whitehead

Play the same as "Klondike" except:

1. Deal all the cards face up.
2. Instead of building in alternate colors, build red on red, black on black.
3. When spaces open up in the layout, fill them with any available card or group of cards.
4. You may only move piles of cards as a unit when the cards are in sequence by suit.

Spiderette

When you're tired of playing "Klondike" and seldom playing out, you might want to get even with this "cheater's version."

The Layout

Lay out the cards the same way you would for "Klondike," but this time, don't set up any foundation piles.

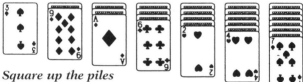

Square up the piles before you play.

The Object of the Game

To build up and then discard all four complete suits.

The Play

Build downward on the layout regardless of suits and colors (but try to build in suit where you can). You can move groups of cards when they are in the correct sequence. When a space opens up in the layout, fill it with any available card or sequence of cards.

When you run out of moves, deal another seven cards onto the layout. At the end, put the last three cards on the first three columns.

Thumb and Pouch

Play the same as "Klondike" except:

1. When building, a card can be laid on any card that is one rank higher, regardless of color, *except* one of its own suit.
2. A space may be filled by any available card or sequence of cards.

The Harp

This is "Klondike" with two packs of cards. Play it the same way as "Klondike," except:

1. Use two packs of cards.
2. Use a nine-card row instead of seven.

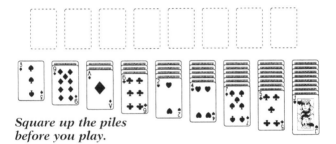

Square up the piles before you play.

3. Go through the cards, one by one until you win or until the game is obviously blocked.
4. When filling a space, you may use an available King, as in "Klondike," or a sequence of cards that has a King at the top.

The Layout

Lay out four cards face up in a row along the top of your playing space, and four cards in a row beneath them—leaving space for a row in between. That's where the foundation will go: two Aces of one color and two Kings of another, as they become available.

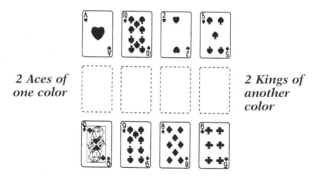

2 Aces of one color

2 Kings of another color

The Object of the Game

Build the Aces in suit to Kings, and the Kings in suit to Aces.

Special Rules

You can move any card from the top row onto the foundations. But you can't move a card from the bottom row unless you can move it straight up into place—into the position directly above its original position.

For example, in the diagram on the left, the 2 of Hearts can go on the Ace of Hearts, but in the diagram on the right, it can't.

2 of Hearts can go straight up onto the Ace, because the Ace is the same suit.

2 of Hearts cannot go onto the Ace, because it is not directly under the Ace of Hearts.

The Play

When you've made all the moves you can to the foundation, deal another four cards to the top and bottom rows. Make your moves and then deal again—until all the cards have been laid out.

At this point the "special rules" no longer apply. You can move any card from the top or bottom rows onto the foundation piles. You can also build top cards from the layout onto each other regardless of suit or color—up or down. Spaces in the layout may not be filled.

Kings may be placed on Aces.

The Layout

Deal five rows of five cards each, so your layout
looks like the diagram below:

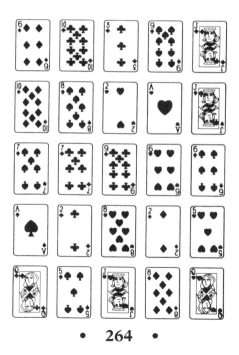

The Object of the Game

To discard the entire deck in pairs of the same rank. You can discard them if they are:

1. Next to each other
2. Above or below each other
3. "Touching" diagonally

The Play

Remove every pair that you can from the layout. When you do, there will be holes. Close up the cards so that all the holes are filled and the cards are in the same order in which you laid them out.

After you make the cards into solid rows again, deal new cards to make up the bottom rows, so that you have five rows of five cards again.

Remove the pairs again in the same way, and when you can't move any more cards, close up the spaces in the layout again, and fill in again from the cards in your hand.

Nestor

The Layout

Deal eight cards faceup in a row. Then deal
another five rows overlapping them, so that you
can see all the rows at one time.

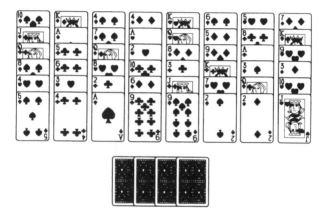

As you deal, make sure you don't have any
cards of the same rank in a column. If you're
about to deal a deuce onto a column that already

has a deuce in it, slip the card underneath the pack and deal another card instead.

You'll have four cards left over when you finish dealing. They are the stock.

The Object of the Game

To discard the whole layout by twos.

The Play

Remove cards of the same rank by twos from the exposed cards at the ends of the columns. When you can't make any more moves, turn up the first card of the stock pile. If that won't help you, turn up the next, and the next.

Osmosis

The Layout

Deal four sets of four cards each facedown. Then square them off, turn the top card faceup, and put them in a column at the left side of your playing space. Place the next card in the deck (which becomes the first foundation) to the right of the top card.

Place additional foundation cards (other cards of the same rank) in a column under the first.

The Object of the Game

Build each foundation card to a full 13 cards, all

of the same suit, regardless of sequence.

Special Rule

No card may be placed in the second, third, or fourth foundation rows unless a card of the same rank has already been placed on the previous foundation card.

The Play

Let's see how this works. In the illustration, the foundation card is the 5 of Hearts. The first thing to do is to build any other Hearts that are already showing, such as the 10 and the King, and put them alongside the 5, overlapping, so you can see what cards have been played to that foundation.

Then start going through the stockpile, three cards at a time, to find additional Hearts and more foundation cards for the other suits.

Let's say you turn up a 5 of Clubs. You place it below the 5 of Hearts.

The next card you turn up is a Queen of Clubs. You cannot place it, because the only cards that have been placed in the Hearts row are the King and the 10. So these are the only Clubs you could put down beside the 5 of Clubs.

Then you get a 10 of Diamonds. You cannot place it next to the 5 of Diamonds, even though there is a 10 of Hearts out on the table, because the 10 of Clubs has not yet been placed.

You get to keep going through the cards until you win the game or until the game is blocked.

Play the same way as "Osmosis," except with the facedown cards turned up and spread so that you can see them all.

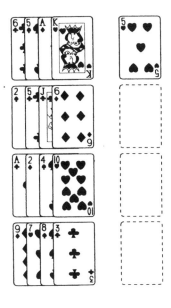

Patience

The Layout

Deal out all four Aces in a row. Underneath each one, deal a card. These cards are the stock from which you are going to build.

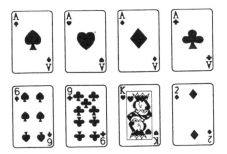

The Object of the Game

To build the Aces up to Kings, regardless of suit.

The Play

When you've finished the moves you can make with the first set of four cards, deal another row of four right on top of them.

For example, in the diagram, you could move the 2 of Diamonds onto the Ace of Diamonds. Then you would deal four cards on top of the cards in the bottom row.

Keep going until you've gone through all the cards.

Tam O'Shanter

Play this game in the same way as "Patience," but don't put the Aces up ahead of time. Wait and put them up when they show up in the deal.

This game is almost impossible to win.

Pyramid

A sad thing about many solitaire games is that you play a round—or five rounds—and then it's over. You have no special feeling of victory (unless you've played out and won), and no way to compare your score to anyone else's.

Here's a game that keeps you counting and scoring all the time. You can play it against yourself, against another player, or against an average score.

The Layout

Lay out the cards in the shape of a pyramid, starting with one card at the top and placing two cards that overlap it, then three overlapping them, and so on, until you have a large triangle with seven cards at its base.

Each card has its own numerical value (face value). Kings count as 13, Queens as 12, and Jacks as 11.

The Object of the Game

To remove the entire pyramid, plus the cards in your hand.

The Play

Your job is to remove pairs of cards that add up to 13 with this catch: You cannot remove a card unless it is exposed—not covered by any other card.

For example, in the pyramid on page 275, you can remove 6 and 7 from the bottom row. This opens up the Ace in the row above, which you can remove with the Queen (worth 12) in the bottom row.

You can remove Kings alone, because they are worth 13 points.

Place all the cards you remove from the pyramid in a special "Removed" pile, faceup. The top card in this pile can be used again to form another 13-match.

Now you start dealing out the rest of the pack one by one. If the card you turn up does not form a match with any card available in the pyramid, put it into a wastepile. Don't mix up this pile with your "Removed" pile.

If one of the cards you turn up from your hand is a match with the top card of the "Removed" pile, you can remove both of them.

You get two re-deals (three times through the cards).

How to Score Pyramid

A match is six games. Score each game as follows:

50 *points:* If you get rid of your pyramid in the first deal (once through the deck).

50 *points minus:* If you get rid of your pyramid in the first deal but still have cards in your hand or in the wastepile, score 50 points minus the number of cards in your hand and the wastepile.

20 *points minus:* If you get rid of the pyramid in the third deal, score 20 points minus the number of cards in your hand or the wastepile.

0 *points minus:* If you never do succeed in getting rid of your pyramid, deduct one point for each card left in the pyramid as well as each card left in your hand and the wastepile. That's right—a minus score!

Average score is 0 for six matches. If you do better, you've won!

Quadrille

The Layout

You don't need to set up the layout for this game ahead of time, which is one of the great things about this game. You put the cards in place as they show up.

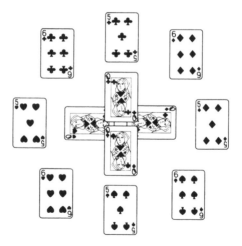

The Object of the Game

To build up the 6s in suit to the Jacks and the 5s down in suit to the Kings.

The Play

Start turning up cards from the deck. As soon as the 5s and 6s appear, put them in place and start building on them. On the 5s you build down:

4   3   2   Ace   King.

On the 6s you build up:

7   8   9   10   Jack.

The queens just sit in the middle and look regal.

You get two re-deals (three times through the cards).

Thirteen

The Layout

Deal a row of five cards.

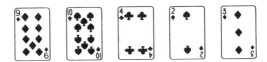

The Object of the Game

To get rid of all the cards.

The Play

Remove any Kings or any pair of cards that adds up to 13. That includes not only:

   3 and 10
   5 and 8
   4 and 9
   6 and 7

but also Ace and Queen—and 2 and Jack.

Discard those cards. Then deal the next row of five cards on top of the first one, and go on removing the cards that add up to 13. You can use only the top cards for pairing and discarding.

When you've gone through the whole pack, you'll have two cards left over. Make them into a separate pile and use them to pair and discard. If you can get rid of all the cards, you've won.

Turkish Delight

In Turkey this is a fortune-telling game. You make a wish before you start. If you win, your wish will come true.

Layout
Deal out the entire deck in thirteen piles of four facedown cards. Turn up the top card of each pile.

The Object of the Game
To get rid of all the cards.

The Play
Remove cards of the same rank in pairs. Every time you remove a card, turn up the card underneath. Continue until all the cards are removed or no move is possible.

The Layout

Place five cards on the table in the shape of a cross. Then place another card in the upper left-hand corner. This is the foundation—the other foundation—the same rank as the corner card—should be placed in the other corners as they come up.

foundation →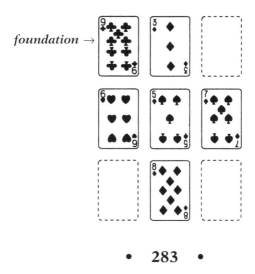

The Object of the Game

To build all the corner cards into four suits.

The Play

Build whatever cards you can onto the foundation, upward in suit. Then build whatever cards you can onto others in the cross—downward and regardless of suit. When you've exhausted all the possibilities, start going through the stockpile one card at a time, playing it to the foundation (going up), to the cards in the cross (going down), or, if unplayable, to a wastepile.

Note: Aces may be placed on Kings.

12
Solitaire with Two or More Decks of Cards

Busy Aces

Play this game with two decks of cards.

The Layout
Deal two rows of six cards each, faceup. Aces, as they become available, are foundations and placed in a row above.

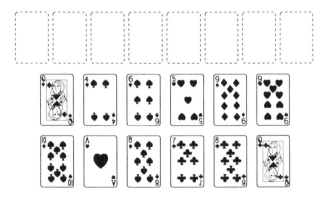

The Object of the Game

Build all eight Aces up in suit to Kings.

The Play

Do whatever building you can at the start on the foundations. Then build on the layout downward and in suit. After you've made all the moves you can, begin turning over cards one by one, discarding unplayable cards onto a wastepile.

When spaces open up in the layout, fill them from your hand or the wastepile.

Congress

You play this game with two decks of cards.

The Layout

Deal a column of four cards to the left and a column of four to the right. Leave enough space between them for the foundations, eight Aces.

The Object of the Game

Build the Aces upward in suit to Kings.

The Play

First make whatever moves you can to the foundations. Then start turning over the cards in your hand one by one, building downward on the layout, regardless of suit, and adding whatever cards you can to the foundations. Fill in spaces from the wastepile or from your hand. Any card on top of a pile is available for building.

Contradance

Play this game with two decks of cards.

The Layout

Select one 5 of every suit and one 6 of every suit.
These are the foundations. Set them up like this:

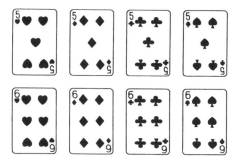

The Object of the Game

Build up the 6s to Queens and the 5s down
(through Aces) to Kings.

Play

Go through the balance of the cards one by one and play them to the foundations in suit wherever you can.

You get one re-deal (twice through the cards).

The Fan

Play this game with two decks of cards.

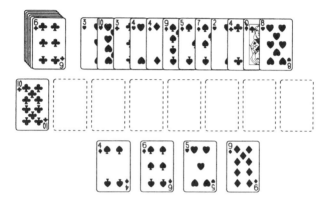

The Layout

First count out 12 cards in one unit. This is the stockpile. Place it faceup at the left. Beside it, place an overlapping string of 12 faceup cards. The next card in your hand will be a foundation card. Let's say it's the 10 of Clubs. Leave space next to it for placing the other 10s—seven more of them—as they come up. They will be foundation cards on which you will build up from 10s through Aces to 9s. Underneath this foundation row, deal out four cards from the pack, faceup.

The Object of the Game

To build all the foundations in sequence, regardless of suits, until they contain 13 cards.

Special Feature

Whether you build up or down on the foundations is up to you. You can make up your mind after you see how the game is shaping up. You don't have to decide until you're ready to start building, but whatever you decide, it will apply to all the foundations.

The Play

Start playing onto the foundations by going through the cards in your hand one by one. Unplayable cards go into a wastepile.

You can also play onto the foundations with the following cards:

1. the top card of the stockpile
2. the exposed card on the end of the string of overlapping cards.
3. the four-card row
4. the top card of the wastepile

If a space opens up in the row of four cards, fill it from the wastepile or the cards in your hand.

You get two re-deals (three times through the cards).

You need two decks of cards.

The Layout

Deal four rows of ten cards each, overlapping, as in the picture. Aces, as they become available, are moved up above the layout as foundations.

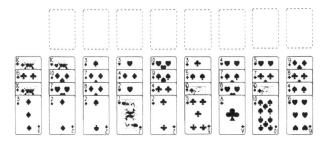

The Object of the Game

Build all eight Aces to Kings in suit.

The Play

First, build what you can to the foundations.

Then build on the layout itself, downward in suit.

For example, in the illustration on page 295, the Ace of Clubs can be played up to the foundation row. So can the 2. The 2 of Diamonds can be placed on the 3 of Diamonds.

When you have exhausted all the possibilities, start going through the cards one by one, building onto the foundations or layout or discarding the unplayable cards into a wastepile. The top card of that wastepile is available too.

When a space opens up in the layout, you can fill it with any card — one from the layout, the top card from the wastepile, or a card from your hand.

Play exactly the same as "Forty Thieves," except build downward on the layout in alternating colors.

Indian

Play exactly the same as "Forty Thieves," except:

1. For the layout, deal 30 cards in three rows of ten cards each. The first row should be face down.
2. When building on the layout, cards may go on any suit except their own.

Lucas

Play exactly the same as "Forty Thieves," except:

1. Set up the Aces in the foundation row before dealing the layout.
2. For the layout, deal three rows of 13 cards each. This makes for a much easier game.

Number Ten

Play exactly the same as "Forty Thieves," except:

1. Place the first to rows face down.
2. Build downward on the layout in alternating colors.
3. When all the cards on the top of a pile are in correct sequence, you're allowed to move them as a unit onto another pile in the layout.

Maria

Play exactly the same as "Forty Thieves," except:

1. For the layout, deal four rows of nine cards each.
2. Build downward on the layout in alternating colors.

Rank and File

Play exactly the same as "Forty Thieves," except:

1. For the layout, deal the first three rows face down.
2. Build downward on the layout in alternating colors.
3. When all the cards on the top of a pile are in correct sequence, you're allowed to move them as a unit onto another pile in the layout.

Miss Milligan

To many, this is the ultimate solitaire game. You need two packs of cards for it.

The Layout
Deal out a row of eight cards. Move all Aces up above the row of cards as they show up. The Aces are foundations.

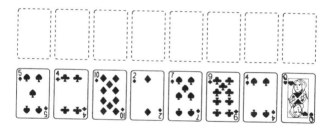

The Object of the Game
Build all eight Aces upward in suit to Kings.

The Play

Besides building on the foundations, you can build within the original row of eight cards—downward in alternating colors.

When you've made all possible moves, deal out another eight cards that overlap the original eight, filling in spaces as you go.

Play off what you can to the foundations, build what you can on the row, and deal another eight cards onto the layout.

You may fill spaces with any available King or with a sequence that leads off with a King.

Continue until you've used up all the cards in your hand. At this point you have the option of "weaving."

Weaving

This is the option of removing one card from the bottom row of the layout temporarily—while you make other moves. When you get that card back into play—either on a foundation or the layout—you are then allowed to remove another card.

You can keep doing this until you win the game or until you can't find a place for the card.

Special Rules

You are permitted to move two or more cards as a unit—when they are built correctly in rank and sequence and at the end of a column.

For example, in the diagram below, you can move the 10 of Diamonds, 9 of Spades, and 8 of Hearts as a unit onto the Jack of Clubs.

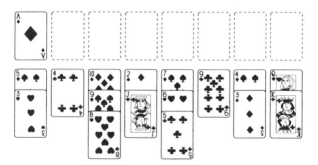

Napoleon's Square

Play this game with two decks of cards.

The Layout

Deal 12 piles of four cards each, four piles to the left (place them horizontally), four to the right (horizontally) and four across the bottom of the layout. All eight Aces will be placed in two rows in the middle of the layout as they show up.

The Object of the Game

Build all the Aces up in suit to King.

The Play

First, make all the moves you can. Move Aces to the foundations and then build on the layout itself, downward and in suit. The top card of any pile is available for building, and so are groups of cards that are in sequence and in the same suit.

When a space opens up in the layout, fill it with any available card or group of cards in sequence and the same suit, or from your hand or the wastepile.

After all initial moves have been made, turn over one card at a time from your hand, discarding unplayable cards to the wastepile. The top card of the wastepile is always available for play.

The Layout

Deal three rows of three cards each. These cards are available for building on the foundations.

The Object of the Game

To build the foundations upward in suit to full 13-card sequences — but you need to do it by 2s! The Aces should build like this:

A 3 5 7 9 J K 2 4 6 8 10 Q

The deuces should build like this:

2 4 6 8 10 Q A 3 5 7 9 J K

The Play

Go through the cards in your hand one by one. When an Ace comes up, start a foundation row above the layout. When a 2 comes up, place it in that row also, as shown in the picture on page 306.

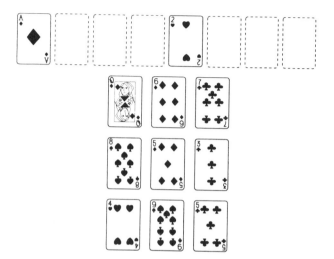

You'll need to place three more Aces and three more deuces in the foundation row, one of each suit. If you can't play the card from your hand onto the foundations, put it in a wastepile. If a space opens up in the group of nine cards, fill it right away from the wastepile or from your hand. You get one re-deal.

This is almost as simple as a game can get, but you need two packs of cards for it.

The Layout

The layout starts with just one card in place, a King. That card will be followed by seven additional cards—the Queen, Jack, 10, 9, 8, 7, and 6 of any suit—as they become available. These are foundations.

The Object of the Game

You need to build each foundation downward and regardless of suit into a sequence of 13 cards.

The Play

Start going through the pack, one card at a time. The catch is that you have to place the Queen before you can put down the Jack, and the Jack must be in place before you can place the 10, and so on, down to the 6. You are free, though, to build on the cards that are already in place.

For example, you can put a Queen on the King that is already on the table, and a Jack on the Queen. Unplayable cards go into a wastepile whose top card is always available.

Kings may be played on Aces, except when the foundation card is something other than an Ace or King.

You get two re-deals (three times through the cards).

# of players: 2-6

There is more action in this card game than in any other that has ever been invented! Actually it isn't a game all on its own, but one that has been put together. You need a pack of cards for every player.

Two or more people play their own games of solitaire, but when they put their Aces up at the top of the spread, *anyone* can build on them! It's an exciting game for three, a wild one for four and if you have enough room (and long arms) you can even go on to six players—and then look out!

The Object of the Game

To be the first one to get rid of all your cards onto the bases (into the middle), or the one to put the most cards into the middle.

The Cards

Everyone needs a deck of cards, and the backs of

each pack must bear a different design or emblem or color from the others, because at the end of the game, the players may have to sort out their own cards in order to see who won. It's also easier to get the packs back together!

What Game?

You can play "Pounce!" with any solitaire game that builds up Aces in suits, but it is most often played with "Canfield" or "Klondike." When playing "Klondike" in a game of "Pounce!," you may run through the deck as many times as you want. "Canfield" makes for a faster game, because the winner is the one who gets rid of the 13-pile first. It doesn't matter where the cards go—into the middle or onto the building piles—as long as they move somewhere.

The Play

Whichever solitaire game you choose, the players lay out their spreads, but no one starts playing until a signal is given. Then, anything goes. Play as fast as you can. Aces that are played to the top of the spread now go in the middle of the table. Try to get as many cards up there as rapidly as you can. These are your points.

In case of a dispute, the player whose card got there first is the one who gets to leave it (that means the card that is lowest in the pile). But it is against the rules to use more than one hand to put cards in the middle. And you can play only one card up there at a time.

The first player to get rid of all his cards wins. But if play comes to a standstill before anyone has gotten rid of his cards, sort out the cards that have made it into the middle: the player with the most cards there wins.

Queen of Italy

Play this game with two decks of cards.

The Layout

Deal 11 cards at the top, overlapping each other, faceup. Then deal three cards faceup—you get the opportunity to choose from these three which one will be your foundation. You make this choice based on the 11 cards you've already laid out.

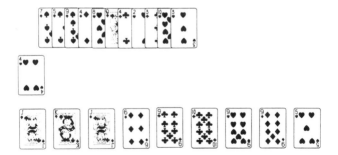

After you decide on a foundation card, put it in

place below and to the left of the first row. Use the two cards you didn't select to start a nine-card row at the bottom. Deal another seven cards from stock. This nine-card row is where the action takes place.

You may play cards to the foundations as they show up. You can also build them on each other downward in alternating colors. Only one card at a time may be moved from the layout.

Kings may be built on Aces, except when your foundation card is an Ace or a King.

What about those 11 cards at the top? They are out of bounds, playable only onto the foundations as they become exposed.

The Object of the Game
Build your foundation cards into eight complete 13-card sequences in alternating colors.

The Play
Start by making what plays you can to the foundations and within the layout. When you can't make any more moves, go through the cards in

your hand one at a time. Play what you can to the foundations and the nine-card row. Put unplayable cards in a wastepile. The top card of the wastepile is always available for play.

Spaces in the nine-card row may be filled from the top card of the wastepile or from the stock pile. Never add any cards to the 11-card overlapping row.

Falling Star

Play in the same way as "Queen of Italy" except:

1. The overlapping row represents stars that have to fall for the game to be won.
2. The next card (the 12th) becomes the foundation.

Blondes and Brunettes

Play the same way as "Queen of Italy" except:

1. Deal only ten cards in the overlapping row instead of 11.
2. The next card (the 11th) becomes the foundation card.
3. Deal nine cards for the bottom row.

Thirteen

Play this game in the same way as "Queen of Italy" except:

1. Deal 13 cards in the overlapping row instead of 11.
2. Build in suit rather than in alternating colors.
3. You do not actually get a re-deal, but you are allowed to turn the wastepile over and play until you reach an unusable card. Then the game is over.

Royal Rendezvous

There's enough variety in this two-deck game to make it fun, even if there are a few surprises!

The Layout

First, lay out all eight Aces in two rows, one on top of the other. Each row should have one Ace of each suit. Then lay out one deuce (2) of each suit—two on each side of the second row, as in the picture. Underneath this row, deal out two rows of eight cards each. They can be played onto the foundations.

The Object of the Game

Build up all eight Aces and four deuces in suit as follows:

1. Build up the top row of Aces in suit to Queens.
2. Build up the bottom row of Aces by twos to Kings, like this:

   A   3   5   7   9   J   K

3. Build up deuces by twos to Queens, like this:

   2   4   6   8   10   Q

4. Put four Kings at the top of the layout, but not until after the other four Kings have appeared in the lowest foundation row.

The Play

Go through the cards, one by one, and build them onto the foundations if you can. If not, discard them to a waste pile. If a space opens up in the bottom two rows, fill it with the top card of the wastepile, or, if there isn't any, with a card from your hand.

St. Helena

With its odd and changing rules, this game is really interesting. Maybe that's why Napoleon is said to have played it while he was in exile. Others say that's unlikely, because the game hadn't even been invented then. There's a lot of laying-out of cards (you need two decks), but it's worth it.

The Layout

Start by removing one Ace and one King of each suit from the cards and setting them up in two rows, Kings on top. These are your foundations.

Then deal out the rest of the pack in 12 piles clockwise: four on top, two on the right side, four underneath the foundations and two on the left side, as in the illustration on page 321.

Keep on dealing, one card on each of the 12 piles, until the cards are all laid out.

The Object of the Game

To build the Aces up in suit to Kings, and Kings down in suit to Aces.

The Play

Only the cards on the tops of the piles can be moved. First, build them onto the foundations; then build them on each other, one card at a time, either up or down, regardless of suit or color. You can reverse direction on the same pile.

When building, only a Queen can go on a King (or vice versa) and only a deuce can go on an Ace.

When you run out of moves, the deal is over.

Special Rules

In the first deal, you are limited in placing cards on the foundations.

1. Only the cards at the sides of the layout can go on any foundation.
2. The cards at the top may be played only to the Kings line.
3. The cards at the bottom may go only on the Aces line. In re-deals (you get two of them), any card of the right suit and rank can go on any foundation. You're not limited in this odd way.

Re-deals

You get two (three times through the cards). To re-deal, gather the piles counterclockwise, starting in the upper left-hand corner. Then deal them out, starting at the left-hand corner, as far as they go.

Louis

Play exactly the same as "St. Helena," except:

1. After you deal the first 12 cards of the piles, play everything you can onto the foundations. Then fill the spaces from the stockpile. After that, deal the rest of the cards.
2. All the cards in the layout can be played to the foundations without any restrictions—in all deals.
3. Building on the layout piles must be in suit.

Play the same way as "St. Helena," except:

1. There is only one deal, with no restrictions on it.
2. Aces can be built on Kings and Kings on Aces.
3. When the top cards of two foundations of the same suit are in sequence, one or more cards may be transferred onto the other foundation. The original Ace and King may not be transferred, though.

Sly Fox

This game calls for two decks of cards.

The Layout

Set out four Aces (one of each suit) vertically at the left, and four Kings (one of each suit) vertically at the right. Then, between them, deal out four rows of five cards.

The Aces and Kings are foundations on which you are going to build.

The Object of the Game

To build the Aces up to Kings, and the Kings down to Aces, by suit.

The Play

Build on the foundations using the cards in the middle of the layout. As each space opens up, fill it with a card from your hand.

When you can't make any more plays, start going through the cards, one by one. If you can play a card onto a foundation, do it. But if you can't, place it on one of the 20 cards that lie between the foundations. You have your choice of which one. As you place it there, count it (do not count the ones that you put on the foundations, though).

When you have placed 20 cards on the 20 cards that lie between the foundations, stop going through the cards. Make any new plays that have become possible in the layout.

Each time play comes to a standstill, start going through the cards again. But this time, don't fill the spaces with cards from your hand. And as before, after you place 20 more "unplayable" cards onto the layout, stop and make all possible moves to the foundations.

Note

There is no limitation on the number of cards that you may play to any card in the layout. You could play all 20 on one card, if you wanted to. Or, you can be sly, like a fox!

Some say that this game is "Sly Fox" in sheep's clothing. It is very similar to that game, and it too calls for two decks of cards.

The Layout

Deal two ten-card rows of cards. Above them, set up a foundation row of four Aces and four Kings, as they show up.

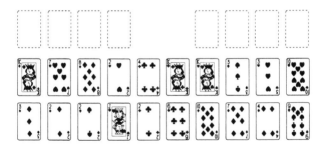

The Object of the Game

To build the Aces up to Kings and the Kings down to Aces in suit.

The Play

First, play whatever you can to the foundations. As spaces open up in the layout, fill them at once with cards from the stockpile.

When you've made every move you can, start playing one card at a time from your hand. If the card can't go on a foundation, you can put it on top of any card in the layout.

No card can be moved off the layout except to place on a foundation.

This two-deck game has been called "the King of all Solitaires."

The Layout

Deal out 54 cards in 10 piles as follows:

> 6 cards in the first four piles
> 5 cards in the last six piles.

Only the top cards should be face up. These piles are the foundations and the layout at the same time, and all the action takes place on them.

The Object of the Game

Build eight sequences in downward order from Kings to Aces right on the layout. Once a sequence is built, it is discarded. So to win the game is to have nothing on the table.

The Play

After you lay out the cards, make all the moves you can, building down, regardless of suit. Note, however, that even though you're permitted to build regardless of suit, you limit yourself when you do it. You are permitted to move a group of cards as a unit only when they are in suit and in correct rank, so while you would never be able to win the game by making only moves that were in suit, it is certainly better to build in suit if you have the choice.

When you move an entire pile, leaving a blank space, you may move any available card or group of cards into it. Keep in mind, though, that a King cannot move, except into a blank space. It cannot be placed on an Ace.

When you can't make any more moves, deal ten more cards, one on each pile, and make whatever moves you can. Follow this procedure for the entire game, dealing another ten cards whenever you're stuck.

All spaces must be filled before you are allowed to deal another ten cards onto the layout.

After you have put together a complete sequence, you don't have to discard it right away. You may be able to use it to help build other sequences.

The Sultan of Turkey

The most delightful aspect of this two-deck game is the way it looks when you win.

The Layout

Remove the eight Kings and one Ace of Hearts from the pack and place them as shown in the illustration. Add four cards from the pack on both sides of the Kings. You can use these cards to build onto the foundations. All the Kings and the Ace are foundations, except for the King of Hearts that is in the middle of the square. Don't build on that.

The Object of the Game

To build all the Kings (except for the middle King of Hearts) up to Queens in suit, and to build the Ace of Hearts to a Queen, also. Of course, in order to build up the Kings, you'll need to add an Ace before starting on the 2s.

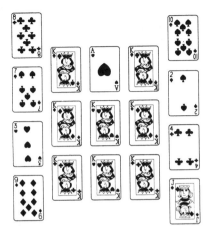

The Play

Go through the cards one by one and start adding to the foundations. Any cards you can't use go into a wastepile.

When a space opens up in the layout, fill it at once, either from the wastepile or from your hand.

You get two re-deals. Shuffle the cards well before going through them a second and third time.

Toad in the Hole

Play this game with two decks of cards. Another name for it is "Frog."

The Layout

Count out 13 cards and place them in one pile faceup. Make sure no Aces are in the pile. If there are, replace them with other cards. Then place one Ace next to the pack as a foundation. As other Aces turn up, place them next to it.

The Object of the Game

Build all the Aces up by suit to Kings.

The Play

Go through the stockpile card by card. When cards are not playable, place them in a row of their own underneath the foundation row. Set up a row of five piles that you will have available for this purpose. You can put the cards in any positions you choose—all in one pile, if you want.

Play the same as "Toad in the Hole" except:

1. Count out only 12 cards instead of 13 for the faceup pile.
2. Do not set up an Ace to start the foundation row.

Two decks of cards are needed for this game.

The Layout

Select from the pack one Ace and one King of each suit. Place them in two rows, Kings on top. These are the foundations.

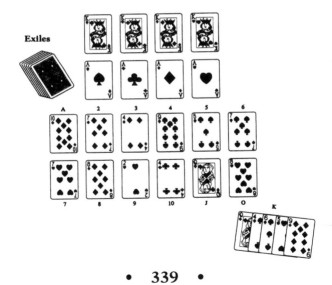

Below them, deal out two rows of six faceup cards each. As you deal them out, count to yourself, "Ace, 2, 3, 4, 5, 6, 7, 8, 9, 10, Jack, Queen, King" (as numbered in the illustration—note that the King is off to the right). If the card you name appears as you name it, that card is an Exile. Put it aside at your left facedown. Deal another card in its place, repeating the same card name. In this way, deal out the entire two decks of cards.

The Play

When all the cards are laid out, build what you can to the foundations. All the top cards of the piles are available plus all the cards in the Kings pile. Spread out the Kings pile so that you can view all the cards.

Then uncover one card from the cards at your left—the Exiles. If the Exile card can be played onto a foundation, you must play it. If it cannot, place it at the bottom of the pile that corresponds to its number. If it is a 3, for example, slip it under the 3s pile. Then take the top card from the

3s pile —let's say it's a Queen—and slip it under the Queens pile. Continue in this way until you can place something on a foundation. If you turn up a King, however, all play stops. Slip the King on the bottom of the Kings pile, and turn up the next Exile card.

Reversal Rule

When the Ace foundation and the King foundation of the same suit are in sequence, you are permitted to shift all the cards from one foundation onto the other.

Let's say, for instance, that you've built the Ace foundation up to the 6 and the King foundation down to the 7. According to this rule, you could move the 6, 5, 4, 3, and the 2 onto the King foundation. You are not allowed, though, to move the original Ace or King.

Re-deals

You get two. To re-deal, gather the cards up beginning with the Kings pile and go backwards through the cards to the Ace pile, so that Kings are on top, Aces on the bottom.

There's plenty of action in this hypnotic game for which you need two decks. Some strategy is also useful.

The Layout

Put an Ace in the middle of the design. Then deal two more cards in each direction in the shape of a windmill. See the diagram on page 344.

The Object of the Game

To build the Kings down to Aces, regardless of suit, and build the Ace up in a continuous sequence (also regardless of suit) until it contains 52 cards—four times through the Ace-to-King sequence.

The Play

Go through the cards in your hand, one by one. As Kings appear, put them in the angles of the windmill, as shown by the dotted lines. They are foundations. Build down on them, regardless of suit.

The central Ace is also a foundation. Build up on it regardless of suit. Put unplayable cards in a wastepile.

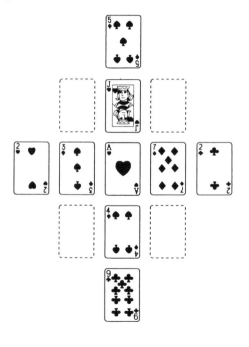

You can use the cards in the windmill shape for foundation building. When a space opens up in the windmill, fill it from the wastepile, or if there is no wastepile, from the cards in your hand.

It is legal to steal the top card from a King foundation to use for the Ace foundation on the following conditions:

1. that you use only one card at a time.
2. that the next card to go on the Ace foundation must come from a regular source.

Glossary

Ante up. To put counters into the pool so that they may be won during the game.

Build. In solitaire, to place one card on another to create a sequence—whatever kind is called for. Usually, the sequence just goes up or down. The Queen, for example, is placed on the King if the sequence is down, on the Jack if it's up.

For a description of building in "Casino," see pages 142–145.

Capot. Trying to win all the tricks.

Column. Cards that go vertically in a line.

Deuce. 2s.

Discard pile. The pile of cards already played or rejected by the players.

Follow suit. Put down a card that matches the suit of the lead.

Foundations. The cards that score—the ones you build on in solitaire. They are usually—but not always—put up above the layout.

Honors. Ace, King, Queen, and Jack of the trump suit in "Whist."

Lead. The first card that establishes the suit to follow.

Meld. To match up three or four cards of a kind or in sequence. Can be held in the hand or put down on the table. A matched set.

Rank. The number of a card. A 10 of Diamonds "ranks" higher than a 9 of Diamonds.

Revoke. Not following suit when you could have and were supposed to.

Row. Cards that go horizontally in a line.

Sequence. Three or four cards of a suit in order.

Set. Three or four cards of the same rank.

Stock. Unplayed cards (the pack) from which a

player may draw a new card or from which the dealer may deal new cards to players.

Suits. Hearts, Diamonds, Clubs, and Spades.

Trailing. Placing a card faceup on the table in "Casino."

Trick. A sequence in which each person plays a card according to certain rules.

Trump suit. A named suit that can overtake others.

Upcard. The top card of the stock, turned up to start the discard pile.

Wastepile. The discarded cards.

Widow. An extra hand or number of cards that may be substituted for a player's own hand or held until a certain point in the game. Also, extra cards taken with the first tricks in Hearts.

Wild cards. Cards that prior to the start of play may be given any value you choose.